JOHN
TERRY

World Cup Heroes:

JOHN TERRY

Oliver Derbyshire

JB

JOHN BLAKE

Published by John Blake Publishing Ltd,
3 Bramber Court, 2 Bramber Road,
London W14 9PB, England

www.johnblakepublishing.co.uk

This edition published in paperback in 2010

ISBN: 978 1 84358 170 3

British Library Cataloguing-in-Publication Data:

A catalogue record for this book is available from the British Library.

Design by www.envydesign.co.uk

Printed in Great Britain by CPI Bookmarque, Croydon, CR0 4TD

1 3 5 7 9 10 8 6 4 2

Papers used by John Blake Publishing are natural, recyclable products
made from wood grown in sustainable forests. The manufacturing processes
conform to the environmental regulations of the country of origin.

Pictures reproduced by kind permission of Clevamedia, Empics
and Getty Images.

1

John George Terry was born on 18 December 1980, the second son of Ted and Sue Terry and a brother for Paul. John forged a close relationship with his big brother as the two lads helped each other on their way to achieving their dreams as professional footballers. They also received a lot of encouragement from their dad who'd had a trial with West Ham in his youth. Ted didn't make the grade but he was a big influence on the boys who watched him play for his local team. 'I remember he was always screaming and shouting,' John recalled. 'People would say how he never stopped talking, so it was something I learnt from him. He was a leader and a centre-half as well.'

After early years with a team called Comet, John moved to Senrab FC. The club was already famous as the breeding ground for some of the southeast's finest players including Ray Wilkins, Sol Campbell, Lee Bowyer, Muzzy Izzett and Ade Akinbiyi. Senrab's formula of top-class coaching and a strict code of conduct that demanded 100 per cent commitment from the boys had clearly worked, and continued to do so. John played in the same team as Ledley King, Paul

Konchesky, Jlloyd Samuel and Bobby Zamora, all of whom went on to be Premiership players.

King recalled: 'John used to be a midfield player because he wasn't that big. He had a growth spurt and shot up, so now he's an obvious choice for centre-back. He was really good in the air even when he was quite short. Even then you could see he had leadership qualities.'

The Senrab captain was Paul Nicholls and Terry is proud to say, 'He has been my best mate throughout. When we were eleven, we were both playing for Comet and then moved to Senrab. We have just stayed together throughout. He was always there for me and he still is now.'

Naturally Senrab games attracted lots of league scouts, and the best youngsters were invited to train with clubs who hoped to sign them on schoolboy terms as soon as they were 14. As a Barking lad, Terry spent a long time with West Ham and he also had a spell with Arsenal and a trial at Manchester United. The 13-year-old was driven to United's famous Cliff training ground by scout Malcolm Fidegeon, and the other passenger in the car was a lad about four years older, from nearby Leytonstone: David Beckham.

Alex Ferguson made it clear he was very keen to get Terry's signature but the youngster had already been training at Chelsea, and that was where he wanted to play. A big factor in his decision was Gwyn Williams, the Chelsea scout and later assistant manager, who took him under his wing. 'My parents couldn't take me to training all the time, so Gwyn would arrange for someone to pick me up and take me home,' Terry explained. 'He would also phone to see how I was, and little things like that meant a lot. Signing

for Chelsea meant leaving Senrab but, like so many of other big names who started there, Terry has never forgotten where it all began and he has been back to make the end-of-season presentation to other 'graduates'.

Leaving the dodgy pitches of Wanstead Flats behind, the first task for the young hopeful was to find his best position. A midfielder all his life, the teenager had great touch and he combined composure on the ball with a fine range of passing, plus an ability to read and control a game. Too short to play at the back, he also lacked pace, though that wasn't a big a problem at that age. Chelsea had actually been uncertain that he would make it because of his size, but then he started to shoot up. One day the youth team were struggling for centre-halves, he filled in and never looked back.

For two years the diminutive Terry combined his studies at Eastbury Comprehensive School in Barking with training at Chelsea. 'I wasn't great at school. It was only in the last year that I really knuckled down because my parents had really drummed it into me,' Terry told *Chelsea TV*. 'I got eight GCSEs but not great grades.'

Off the pitch Terry was just one of the crowd but, on the other side of the white line, he was a natural leader. He got plenty of experience as captain, even with the Chelsea youth, but he had to be careful about his weight. 'I was short and fat when I was younger. When I first signed I still had a bit of puppy fat. But by about 18 or 19 I was fully developed.'

Chelsea, too, were changing. The carefree attitude of old passed when Ken Bates rescued the debt-ridden club, buying it for £1 in 1982. He saw them safely out of the old Division

Two and, although they slipped down again briefly in 1988, they returned to the top flight at the first attempt. When Terry agreed to join Chelsea in 1994 they were on the up under their recently appointed manager, Glenn Hoddle.

With millions of pounds of television money pouring into the Premiership and the Blues receiving further investment from Matthew Harding in 1994, the biggest names in world football were now viewing England with interest. And suddenly Chelsea had a big-name manager of whom the top players had heard, which made them a very attractive proposition indeed.

2

As Terry worked his way through his apprenticeship in the youth and reserve teams, he got to train with some of the game's biggest names including Dutch ace Ruud Gullit and former Manchester United striker Mark Hughes. 'It was great at the time,' Terry said on the *FA website*. 'Hughes was a legend to us and all the YTS boys were fighting for his autograph. I was a Man United fan when I was growing up and he was my hero. So to get a chance to play against him in training and to play with him was fantastic.'

Hoddle took over from Terry Venables as England manager after Euro 96, but Gullit slipped seamlessly into his shoes and the big names continued to make their way to Chelsea. Gianluca Vialli, Frank Leboeuf, Roberto Di Matteo and Gianfranco Zola all arrived in 1996 and played a key part in the club's FA Cup Final victory over Middlesbrough the following year. Edging closer and closer to the first-team squad and on his way to a professional contract, Terry needed to find himself an agent. He turned to Aaron Lincoln.

'I first met him when I was a kit boy and he was the kit man. The thing I liked about him was that he was the same with everybody, whereas some people would be different if the manager or someone else was around. He would sometimes watch a youth game I was in and would tell me if I was crap, which is the sort of thing you need to hear. At other times, he would do the opposite and tell me if I was good. We are probably best mates.'

Chelsea continued to grow on the pitch and Terry watched enviously as his senior club-mates picked up more silverware in 1998. Now under the management of Vialli, they won a cup 'Double', first beating Middlesbrough in the League Cup, and then VfB Stuttgart 1–0 in the European Cup Winners' Cup Final. Yet more big names arrived at Chelsea. Playing regularly as a centre-back, Terry now found two World Cup-winning defenders in Marcel Dessailly and Frank Le Boeuf blocking his way to the first team. But the young Englishman, still only 17, was just excited at the prospect of training alongside such great players.

'When I finished training with the youth team, I would go over and watch the first team for an hour,' Terry recalled. 'I would watch Marcel Desailly and Frank Leboeuf, and then go and try the things they were doing. That improved my game. The first couple of times I trained with the first team, I asked them loads of questions. They were looking at me and thinking: 'Little kid, give it a rest.' But it paid off. They would spend 10 minutes with me, advising me how to position myself when the attacker approached. They told me always to stay on my feet as long as possible, always to watch the

ball rather than the attacker's legs. To learn off two World Cup winners was brilliant.'

The first time Terry trained with the big boys he made a memorable impression on his new boss, clattering the shaven-headed striker to the ground with all the enthusiasm of youth. Under many managers such actions may have brought a punishment, but Vialli thought here was a player with no fear, no respect for reputation. Terry continued to train with the first team and turn in solid performances for the reserves. It was only a matter of time before his chance came.

'I was training with the first team as a centre-back when Luca said he was short of a right-back, and asked if I would play there. He told me: "Go and do the best you can. Just enjoy it."' It wasn't his favourite position but Terry finally got his chance to pull on the blue shirt of Chelsea on Wednesday, 28 October 1998, against Aston Villa in the third round of the League Cup at Stamford Bridge. He received a mixed reception.

The crowd roared their approval when they saw that a young Englishman was about to make his debut in his now famous number 26 shirt. The hardcore fans had heard that the reserve team captain had real ability and they were looking forward to seeing him, but one of his team-mates wasn't so happy. Terry came on after 86 minutes for Dan Petrescu, and the Romanian full-back was so upset that he refused to shake hands with his replacement and then he slapped away the water bottle offered him, before throwing down his track-suit top and kicking the dugout.

But this was little more than a passing irritation for

Terry as he strode out across the Stamford Bridge turf to make his first-team debut. The game became safe in the 85th minute after Vialli completed his hat-trick, making it 4–1. There was still life left in the game though as Dennis Wise was sent off for a rash two-footed lunge on Villa's Darren Byfield. Terry kept his cool in the ensuing fracas, and stayed clear when Vialli got involved in an argument with the Villa bench. Everybody was pleased to hear the final whistle after such a fraught end to proceedings, especially Petrescu who had calmed down and sought out the teenage debutant to make an apology for his display of petulance.

The media didn't give Terry much chance of breaking into the side regularly. With all the big-name signings, a number of talented graduates of Chelsea's academy had been forced to move elsewhere to get first-team football. The youngster was still far from the finished article but Vialli kept him involved with the squad, and he was on the bench a couple of times, including at Spurs the day after his 18th birthday, when Chelsea went to the top of the league for the first time since November 1989.

On Boxing Day, against Southampton, Terry appeared in central midfield for the last 20 minutes of a 2–0 win. The three points re-established Chelsea at the top of the league and coach Graham Rix said: 'We have come to places like this in years gone by and struggled. Today, we more or less controlled it. From World Cup winner Leboeuf to the 17-year-old boy Terry, they're all pulling in the same direction.' The coach may have got the age wrong but Terry was just happy to be involved.

One week later he made his first start in the FA Cup, in

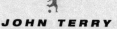

the third round at Oldham, again showing his versatility by completing 90 minutes at right-back. Vialli struck two more cup goals to ensure a 2–0 win. Against a Division Two side in a typical cup-tie, Terry was as composed as ever and did a fine job in what was a pretty scrappy affair.

After seeing his worth in that match, the Blues boss selected Terry at right-back again in the fourth-round match at Oxford United. Since Chelsea were at the top of the Premiership and unbeaten in the league since an opening-day defeat to Coventry, they were the undisputed favourites against a side struggling against relegation from the First Division. Perhaps they were also starting to believe their own hype because they were very fortunate to head back down the M40 still in the competition after salvaging a draw with a controversial injury-time penalty.

Terry found himself back on the bench for the replay as Chelsea fought back from a goal down to take a 4–1 lead. With the game safe, Vialli gave the teenager a chance to play in his preferred position. After 59 minutes Leboeuf made way and the teenager played the final half hour alongside Desailly. The match finished 4–2 but there was little the young centre-back could have done about the goal, as Wise foolishly handled in the area and Dean Windass converted the penalty.

Despite another commendable display from the bench, first-team action was sparse for the remainder of the season and, barring a couple of appearances, Terry had to make do with games in the reserves and occasionally the youth team. He was often handed the captain's armband and was happy to play for either side. However, before the season was out, he got his first taste of European action, starting at full-back against Valerenga. Defending the European Cup Winners' Cup, Chelsea travelled to Oslo with a 3–0 lead from a comfortable first leg and soon destroyed the Norwegians faint hopes of a revival by scoring twice in the opening 15 minutes. Terry made the first goal for his manager when he whipped a low cross to the far post, and Vialli lashed it into the roof of the net at the second attempt. The Blues were in control throughout a game that ended 3–2 to the visitors, despite the home side's valiant attempts to get an equaliser right up until the final whistle.

However, Real Mallorca proved too good in the semi-finals and Chelsea crashed out of the FA Cup to Manchester United in the quarter-finals. Wimbledon had already stopped the Blues in the League Cup and now both Arsenal and United had raced ahead in the Premiership. A season that had promised so much drew to a close with only the European Super Cup a testament to the supremely talented squad assembled at the Bridge.

Assured of third place in the league, Vialli rotated his squad for the last game of the season and Terry appeared as a substitute when Chelsea finished the campaign with a 2–1 win over Derby County, replacing Michael Duberry after 57 minutes. After a long season on the edge of the first team, it was Vialli's way of thanking the youngster for all his hard work, and a tribute to his professionalism.

Even better, Terry was named Chelsea's Young Player of the Year by the fans who recognised the huge potential in the young stopper and, despite only three first-team starts and four substitute appearances in a season of 56 matches, the Stamford Bridge faithful liked what they saw.

Chelsea finished third with 75 points, three points behind Arsenal and four behind Manchester United. It was their highest league finish since 1977 and secured them a place in the Champions League qualifying round. Luca Vialli hung up his boots to bring down the curtain on a stellar career, but the season had seen the arrival of a young player who would prove to be vital to Chelsea's future.

3

'I wasn't really expecting to be ready for the first team until I was 22,' Terry once told the *Sunday Times*. 'Maybe if I hadn't got into the first team by then I'd have looked elsewhere, but until then I was prepared to be patient.' He had to be. The French trio of Desailly, Leboeuf and Lambourde stood between him and a first-team place. Vialli had faith in Terry but, as a young manager in a high-profile job, he needed experienced performers with an impending campaign in club football's premier competition – the Champions League.

Chelsea went through their pre-season friendlies unbeaten and Terry was involved in most of the games until he picked up an injury, which put him out of action for the whole of August. He finally made his first senior appearance of the season in October as Vialli continued his policy of resting his top players in the League Cup, but the youngster found himself on the wrong end of a 1–0 defeat by Huddersfield Town.

Chelsea were proving inconsistent. The European players flourished in the Champions League but struggled in the blood and thunder of the Premiership. Matters came to a head in a 4–1 defeat at Sunderland. Terry brought some of the 'bulldog spirit' back to the Blues in the second half as Desailly made way for him with a thigh injury but, by then, they had already conceded four goals. He came off the bench again the following Saturday in what proved a much easier match. Terry replaced Hogh after an hour as Chelsea proved they had fire in their bellies, beating Hull City 6–1 at Boothferry Park. But Chelsea's Premiership aspirations took another dent the following weekend as Leeds maintained their top spot with a 2–0 win.

The defeat by Leeds was further complicated by injuries to Desailly and Hogh, along with a red card shown to Leboeuf. With three centre-backs out of action, Terry hoped for a call up but instead Vialli swooped to buy Emerson Thome from Sheffield Wednesday. The Brazilian made his debut on Boxing Day and Terry watched from the substitutes' bench as Chelsea fielded the first-ever all-foreign starting line-up in English football.

Even with the signing of Thome, though, Chelsea were still short of players at the back and, at Valley Parade on Saturday, 8 January 2000, John Terry made his full Premiership debut. He didn't enjoy a great beginning as Bradford City went 1–0 up inside a minute. But he came close to his first Chelsea goal two minutes later as he shinned a Wise corner against the bar. Matthew Clarke was in inspired form in the Bradford goal, and he made countless fine saves as Chelsea continued to carve out chances. The pick of them was a remarkable stop at full stretch when Terry met a Wise free-kick with a firm header. There was to be no debut goal for Terry and it took a cool

finish from Dan Petrescu to beat the seemingly superhuman keeper. Chelsea were now seventh in the table, a massive 12 points behind Leed.

With Desailly out injured, Terry had another chance four days later when Chelsea entertained Spurs in the Premiership. The Blues took all three points thanks to a fine debut from George Weah, the Liberian former World, European and African Footballer of the Year. Left out for the next match, Terry returned for the visit of Nottingham Forest in the FA Cup. His first-team appearances were mainly confined to that competition as Thome was cup-tied after playing in an earlier round for Sheffield Wednesday. Chelsea put in a decent performance against the Division One strugglers to win 2–0.

Against Leicester City in the fifth round Terry slipped into the action at half-time, and Chelsea battled their way into the quarter-finals at the expense of Martin O'Neill's combative side. He again came close to scoring but his header cannoned back off the bar from another Wise corner. He also impressed by the way he dealt with the physical presence of Emile Heskey and Matt Elliott, playing up front. Oliver Holt said *The Times*: 'John Terry, a home-grown rarity, looked assured beyond his years at centre-half.'

Chelsea were showing no signs of weakness in the FA Cup and, in the quarter-final, they made quick work of Gillingham, thrashing them 5–0. The second came from the head of Terry, his first senior Chelsea goal. Having come close to scoring a couple of times, it was a great moment for the young defender when he met Gianfranco Zola's corner from six yards out and powered the ball past Vince Bartram.

The goal was all too much for one man inside Stamford Bridge that Sunday afternoon. Ted Terry sat weeping tears of joy. 'My dad was so proud that he started crying in the East Upper stand when everyone was celebrating,' Terry said. 'My mum cried too when I spoke to her on the phone later. My dad is not an emotional guy and I was quite surprised when he told me. His mate, who was there with him, said he'd never seen my dad cry until then.'

Even after his goal against the Gills, the youngster returned to the reserve team and the manager chose two from Desailly, Leboeuf and Thome. When Hogh returned from injury in March to complete a full house of centre-backs for the Blues, Vialli decided to help out an old friend and sent Terry to Nottingham Forest on loan until the end of the season. David Platt's side were struggling in Division One following their relegation from the Premiership at the end of the previous season. Their defence desperately needed shoring up.

On transfer deadline day, Platt swooped for Manchester City's Tony Vaughan and Terry in a bid to stop a second consecutive drop. Before his arrival in Nottingham, Terry's new team-mates had picked up two points from four games and were just two places off relegation. Things got worse for Platt's side when Blackburn left the City Ground with three points. Terry watched from the stands just days after joining the battle for survival.

His First Division experience started when he played the last half hour against the champions elect. Charlton Athletic travelled north knowing that they were only four points away from promotion to the Premiership but, thanks to Terry, they returned home only one point better off. When Terry came off the bench the Addicks were 1–0 up, and things became more difficult for the youngster when his fellow centre-back Colin Calderwood received his marching orders 10 minutes later. With only 20 minutes to play Charlton should have been home and dry, but the red card inspired Forest and they snatched a point thanks to a Chris Bart-Williams penalty in the 81st minute.

In his next match Terry helped his new side to only their fourth away win of the season, beating Birmingham City 1–0 thanks to a Darren Purse own goal. There was a perfect blend of youth and experience in the Forest defence as Terry forged a resolute partnership with the Scottish veteran Calderwood. The double-act came to an unfortunate end early in the second half as the former Spurs centre-back broke his ankle in a collision with one of the Birmingham midfielders. But Terry held firm alongside Jon-Olav Hjelde for the rest of the match and the whole of the next game against Sheffield United, which finished 0–0 as Forest maintained their unbeaten run. Meanwhile Chelsea had reached the FA Cup Final by beating Newcastle 2–1 at Wembley, but had crashed out of Europe after losing 5–1 to Barcelona in the Nou Camp.

Forest's Division One survival was guaranteed at Craven Cottage with a 1–1 draw on Easter Monday. After securing safety, Forest played some of their best football of the season to beat Port Vale 2–0 at home, and the last game of the campaign was a typical end-of-year affair as chances came thick and fast against Stockport County in an entertaining 3–2 win. Terry had played six games, starting five, as Forest won three and drew three, and the Chelsea starlet was certain they had turned the corner and might even be in with a chance of promotion the following season.

Platt was keen to sign Terry to help with this bid, but Chelsea rejected all his advances and the defender returned to Stamford Bridge for the climax to the Blues' season. Back in the Premiership, Terry made the bench for the last league game of the season, replacing Desailly after 55 minutes. It was an enjoyable run-out for the youngster as Chelsea treated their fans to some exhibition football. Derby were 2–0 down when Terry came on and the game finished 4–0 to give the players a confidence boost ahead of the FA Cup Final.

On Saturday, 20 May 2000, Chelsea won the last FA Cup Final at the old Wembley Stadium. The game against Aston Villa was billed as a battle between England and the Rest of the World, as John Gregory had built his squad with players mainly from the British Isles, in contrast to Vialli who had fielded an entirely foreign side on Boxing Day and regularly had only one or two Englishmen in his starting line-up.

Dennis Wise was the only Brit to start for the Blues at Wembley, but there was a more English feel to the bench with Terry completing a trio of home-grown players alongside Harley and Morris. Having already made FA Cup history with the fastest-ever goal in a final after just 43 seconds in 1997, Roberto Di Matteo hit another landmark strike, the last Cup Final goal at Wembley before its renovation. When David James failed to hold Zola's free-kick in the 73rd minute, Di Matteo was on hand to lash the ball home from close range and become a Wembley hero for the second time in three years. Terry claimed his first

medal. He may not have appeared in the final but he certainly played his part in getting his side there, having been involved in the third, fourth and fifth rounds, and the sixth when he claimed his first senior Chelsea goal.

Vialli had always stressed the need for experience and the Chelsea chairman Ken Bates clearly agreed because, for all the youthful manager's enthusiasm, spirit and desire, he was still short of experience, and with the FA Cup freshly stored away in the Stamford Bridge trophy cabinet it came as a shock to everyone, including Terry, when the manager was sacked after only five league games of the new season.

4

The extraordinary thing about the manger's sacking was that Ken Bates hd already allowed Gianluca Vialli to spend heavily on strengthening his FA Cup-winning squad. They beat Manchester United 2–0 at Cardiff's Millennium Stadium to win the Charity Shield and then put four goals past West Ham at the Bridge. There were still rumours that the dressing room was unhappy with the manager, and a 2–0 defeat at Bradford reminded people of the inconsistency which had plagued them the previous seasons. One week later Vialli's side let a 2–0 lead slip against Arsenal at the Bridge for the second time in 12 months – this time handing them a 2–2 draw – and the manager's fate was sealed.

Claudio Ranieri took charge of a team 17th in the table with six points from six games and a squad filled with the previous manager's signings. Terry was recovering from an ankle injury as the results started to go against the Blues, but Howard Wilkinson had seen enough good work from the young defender in the previous season to include him in the England Under-21 squad for a friendly against

Georgia. The Chelsea youngster missed the game through injury but his selection proved that his performances had been noted by people outside Stamford Bridge, and by people that mattered.

As the man who had given Zola his big break at Napoli all those years before, Ranieri had a good eye for talent and he wasn't afraid to give younger players a chance – surely music to the ears of Terry. 'I remember we had a reserve game against Coventry,' the defender recalled on Chelsea TV. 'We won 3–2 and there was a lot of talk about the new manager coming to watch the game with all his staff. I just remember Ray Wilkins coming up to me before the game and telling me to just do the same as I had been doing all season in training: go out and impress him. That is what I did.'

Terry was very impressive in that game, and further good news came his way from the mouth of his new manager, although admittedly English wasn't his best language. Speaking through a translator, Ranieri said, 'I need to have a close look at what I have got before spending money. I want to keep everyone who loves Chelsea. I have told them that big names and reputations mean nothing to me, only performances. I don't look at names, just how they play. I will be treating the youth team players just the same as the reserves and first-team stars. They will all be given a chance.'

As far as Terry was concerned, the new man was saying all the right things and it got better. 'The backbone has to be English,' Ranieri continued. 'If a team in Italy wins the championship, the backbone is Italian. The same happens in Spain. I must evaluate what players I have got and what

English players to buy. I need to see if there are any good English players here. It is impossible for me to say what is going to happen this season. My first job is to get the team to step up another gear. It is obvious morale has been affected by what happened.' That morale was boosted by a 3–3 draw at Old Trafford but suffered yet another blow with a humiliating 2–0 defeat in Zurich to put the Blues out of the UEFA Cup. Terry was sidelined by a hamstring injury for these games and had to wait for his chance to show the new boss what he could do in the first team.

In the meantime the Chelsea centre-back made his England Under-21 debut in a 2–2 draw with Finland. He almost helped his team to three points in their European Under-21 Championship qualifier, but volleyed a Michael Carrick corner just over the bar in the dying seconds. The West Ham midfielder was a regular at Upton Park despite his tender years, and he felt sympathy for Terry at Chelsea, comparing him to another of England's talented young centre-backs, Rio Ferdinand.

Carrick told a press conference: 'Rio had a chance to prove himself at West Ham but other clubs just buy World Cup winners which puts you down the pecking order a bit. What chance would Rio have had at Chelsea? I speak to John Terry and I can understand his frustration at being at Chelsea where young players don't get a chance. Rio got into the West Ham side at 17 and played at the top level for five years. It makes me realise how lucky I am at West Ham.'

Terry had the opportunity to stake his claim for a place in the Chelsea first team soon after his international bow, when Ranieri used the League Cup to see some of his less celebrated players in action for the first time. Playing Liverpool away in the third round, the defender showed his new boss sufficient promise to keep his place in the starting line-up for the league game against Southampton at the Dell. And although Chelsea lost both games, Ranieri liked what he saw. A thigh strain kept Terry out of three games for the Blues and one for England Under-21, but when he recovered the fine young stopper returned to the Chelsea defence and started 10 consecutive matches, which established him as a first-team regular.

Skipper Dennis Wise was full of praise for the youngster. 'We've got a lot of young talent at the club and they've all done extremely well,' he said. 'The way John Terry performed you'd have thought he had played a lot of first-team games, but he hasn't. It's nice to have the youngsters playing. Some of us are getting on a bit and can't play as many games as we'd like to, but we've got good youngsters capable of coming in and doing well.'

Chelsea's season was being wrecked by horrendous away form. They had been knocked out of the UEFA and League Cups and had lost six and drawn four matches in the league, real relegation form. Their continued excellence at home, where they had won seven and drawn two of their 10 league matches, meant that in fact the Blues were 10th in the table but this wasn't acceptable for a team like Chelsea. The press laid the blame squarely at the feet of the new manager and his excessive number of tactical changes that made it difficult for the players to maintain any momentum.

However, Terry was happy with the progress he was making under the new regime, and Ranieri clearly had faith in the young Englishman as he rotated Leboeuf out of the starting line-up for the FA Cup third-round tie against Peterborough. The Blues boss reverted to a more simple formation with four at the back for the visit of lower-league opposition and the change paid off with a 5–0 win. Terry's stock was continually rising and his valuable performances on the pitch brought the first of many 'TERRY'S ALL GOLD' headlines, as well as the more straightforward 'TERRY-FIC!'

His new status as Chelsea's second-choice centre-back, behind the still imperious Desailly, was further enhanced by a performance at Highbury. After dominating the first-half Arsenal were unlucky to take only a 1–0 lead into the break, but Ranieri changed his side for the second 45 minutes and the Blues emerged with a deserved point in a 1–1 draw. At the start of the match, Terry was in a back three, between Leboeuf and Desailly, but after the interval Chelsea changed to a back four and tellingly it was Leboeuf and not Terry who made way, and the youngster rewarded his manager with his first league goal. Wise whipped in a corner and David Seaman in the Arsenal goal got tangled up with his own defender as Gudjohnsen got his head to the ball. It appeared to go over the line before Lee Dixon and Silvinho tried to clear, but Terry was on hand to nod it into the net.

'It was definitely my goal,' confirmed Terry after the game. 'I'm claiming it. It was a bit of a scramble, but I made sure. Yes, we were better in the second half when we changed our shape. But it was the manager's decision; we just get on with it. That's my eighth consecutive game and I feel more relaxed and part of the team now. The players are making me feel welcome. The new manager is giving the youngsters a chance. Of course it's difficult to come through with so many great players at the club but you get to train with them and learn from them and, when you get your chance, you just have to try and take it.'

Terry was taking all the opportunities to come his way, and his team-mates were as impressed as the media. 'John did get a bit down when he was not in the side and I had to talk to him a lot,' Desailly said in the *Sun*. 'I was always talking to him in training, encouraging him and telling him: "You are the present and the future." Now his time has come, and this Arsenal game was a huge test for him. They have some magnificent forwards and it was his best game for us. He's played well before, but in games against lesser teams. This was a tough one because he hadn't come up against really quick players like Thierry Henry and Sylvain Wiltord, but he proved he could handle it. He needs experience, but John can go all the way to the top. Once he plays for England, I'll be really happy for him. For now, it would be a good idea to get him into the England set-up, like we do with lots of our youngsters in France.'

5

Before Terry could make the step up to the full international side, he needed to negotiate a new contract to reflect his enhanced standing in the Chelsea squad. The deal, signed in October 2000, gave him a basic wage of £5,000 a week, well below the team average, but it included a clause guaranteeing negotiations on a new contract after 20 first-team starts. The youngster said to the *Sun*: 'Once I make those 20 starts, then it's up to me and the club to negotiate something that we're both happy with. Hopefully something will get sorted out as I'd love to stay here. Life just could not be better for me at the moment as I'm really enjoying myself on and off the pitch.'

Chelsea notched a first away win of the season when they were drawn against Gillingham for the second successive year in the FA Cup. After going 3–0 up, everything became a bit tense as the Gills pulled it back to 3–2, but the Blues stood firm and claimed a late goal to win 4–2. Having started 10 consecutive matches, a heavy cold interrupted Terry's first-team run but, while on the sidelines, he struck a new four-and-a-half-year deal with the club worth approximately £15,000 a week. 'I am delighted to pledge my future to Chelsea and hope to achieve a great deal of success with the club,' Terry said.

Terry returned, fit and raring to go, for the visit of Manchester United, his first match against the team he had supported as a boy and whom he had rejected as a 14-year-old. He put in another outstanding performance at the centre of a three-man defence and the Blues took a point off Alex Ferguson's side. Under the scrutiny of the new England manager, Sven-Goran Eriksson, the Chelsea defender looked the most accomplished of the back three with his handling of Ole Gunnar Solskjaer and Andy Cole in the 1–1 draw. And by eclipsing the equally talented, Wes Brown, at the other end, Terry further enhanced calls for inclusion in the Swede's first squad. But the Chelsea defender felt the press were getting a bit overexcited. 'Of course I want to go all the way,' he said to the *Independent on Sunday*. 'But all that England talk's got a bit out of proportion. I'd be happy just to be selected for the Under-21s. I'm still looking over my shoulder – I don't feel that I've achieved anything yet. I don't think I will until I've played twenty or thirty games on the bounce.'

Chelsea were in ninth place in the table in mid-February with no chance of the title, but they still had the FA Cup to defend. After two ties against lower-league opposition, they were drawn away to Arsenal in the fifth round. Facing Henry and Dennis Bergkamp in the home side's attack, Terry and Desailly had their hands full from the start but they managed to keep the Gunners at bay for the first half. But they couldn't keep them out forever, and Henry scored from the spot after Jesper Gronkjaer clattered into Lauren.

It was the first goal Henry had claimed against Terry, and the two would develop quite a rivalry over the coming seasons. 'Henry's world class,' Terry said. 'I realised how good he was from seeing him on television, but there were a few things that you can't really see on TV – a few of his runs were unbelievable.' Henry was often the star for Arsenal, but another brilliant game from Terry meant that the Frenchman's only real opportunity came from the penalty spot. Matt Dickinson, in *The Times*, described Terry as 'Chelsea's one outstanding performer' but even he couldn't stop Sylvain Wiltord's brace, which made it 3–1 after Hasselbaink had scored a thunderous gem to level the scores.

It had been a fine showing in the face of adversity, but it wasn't enough to keep the Blues in the cup and it wasn't enough to get Terry into Eriksson's inaugural England squad. The centre-backs ahead of him in the Swede's thoughts were: Manchester United's Wes Brown, Rio Ferdinand at Leeds, Sol Campbell at Spurs, Liverpool's Jamie Carragher and Ugo Ehiogu of Middlesbrough.

Still only 20, the Barking-born defender was selected for the Under-21s though with a number of other promising youngsters. Terry struggled in the first half of their friendly with Spain, and was replaced at the interval with the score at 2–0. The second goal came after 30 minutes when he was involved in a dreadful mix-up with goalkeeper Paul Robinson, and the Chelsea centre-back didn't come out after the break.

Following such a calamitous display and after such a long run in the team, Chelsea's Italian manager took the opportunity to give his youngster a break, and Terry started the next three matches on the bench. He played only the last five minutes as the Blues finally broke their away duck in the league, beating West Ham 2–0 at Upton Park. Having waited so long for an away win, they should have used it as a springboard from which to launch a late surge up the table to claim a Champions League spot, but instead they twice threw away the lead at home to Sunderland in their next match and lost 4–2. Terry replaced Leboeuf 20 minutes from time with the game at 3–2, and the Frenchman's Chelsea career was effectively over as he picked up a groin injury during the ensuing international break.

Terry again joined up with his England Under-21 colleagues where Howard Wilkinson recognised the defender's natural leadership abilities. With the usual skipper, Blackburn's David Dunn, out injured, the Chelsea centre-back was given the honour of leading out his country against Finland at Barnsley's Oakwell ground. He was Man of the Match in the eyes of most observers and he capped a fine defensive display with the second goal in a 4–0 win, heading in Jonathan Greening's free-kick after 75 minutes. Terry was thrilled with the result. 'A lot of people had a go at us after we lost 4–0 to Spain in the last game,' he said after the game, 'but we always said that was a learning process for us. We showed how much we learned from it and responded well. It was a real honour to be asked to skipper the side, and getting the goal just rounded everything off. I am delighted.'

The coach was also pleased with the performance of his team, and his captain in particular. 'I made Terry skipper for the first time and he played a captain's game. I am delighted for him,' Wilkinson said. 'We looked like a team and, hopefully, we can carry that to Albania on Tuesday.' Terry maintained his one 100 per cent record in charge of the troops as they beat Albania 1–0 with a Greening penalty in Tirana, and he returned to Stamford Bridge in far finer fettle than after his previous Under-21 break.

The Blues began climbing up the table at the business end of the season. With Terry restored to the side, Chelsea won four on the bounce and the previously slim chance of a UEFA Cup place started to look safe. Ever the optimist, Terry aimed his sights higher. 'The Champions League is a real possibility now,' he said. 'For so long it didn't look like we'd be playing in Europe at all next season, but while everyone has ignored us, we've sneaked up on the rails.' Chelsea weren't quite sneaky enough to climb into third place, though, and defeat at Elland Road at the end of April effectively ended their hopes of Champions League football for the following season.

Rumours were circulating that Leboeuf was set to return to France and Terry told the press: 'It's good news for me if Frank leaves because in football you always have to think about your own prospects. Maybe it's a good move for Frank, too. I'm sure the lads will be upset to see him go because he's done well for Chelsea but I have to think about myself. I'm enjoying playing in the first team. The manager told me to be patient and I've taken my chance.'

Terry seemed to be improving with every game and praise was coming from all quarters. Chelsea's assistant manager Gwyn Williams, who played such a key role in the defender's decision to join the Blues, said, 'We believe that what we have in the club is another Tony Adams. They have the same approach to football, the same attitude. Ever since we converted him into a defender, he has shot up in height as if that was just what he was waiting for. But he can play; there are no doubts about that.'

One man who agreed with Williams was Adams himself. 'I love John Terry. He's a fabulous player,' the Arsenal captain said. 'I just hope he gets the guidance that he needs. He was my young player of the year. He could become one of the best centre-backs this country has ever produced.'

Steven Gerrard pipped Terry in the PFA Young Player of the Year award, but the praise from his idol was a phenomenal boost to Terry's confidence. 'Tony Adams is one of the players I've always looked up to,' he said. 'I've always admired the way he's played. He's just brilliant. If I get the chance to watch him play, I always take it. It's wonderful he's said something like that about me.'

Chelsea's campaign drew to a close with a battling 2–2 draw against Liverpool at Anfield, where Hasselbaink twice equalised goals from England's Michael Owen, and the result set Chelsea up to claim sixth spot in their final game of the season at Maine Road. 'From my point of view I found it very difficult trying to mark Michael Owen, but I'm not the first man to have discovered that,' Terry said. 'It was a battling performance, the lads are delighted: we've come back twice and a draw was a good result. Now we need to get a win in our final game at Manchester City to make sure of the UEFA Cup place we all need.' That place was secured with a 2–1 win and Terry's season was almost over.

Just two games for the England Under-21s stood between the young defender and his richly deserved summer holiday.

The first was a friendly against Mexico and the second a European Championship qualifier against Greece. Wilkinson's previous skipper, David Dunn, had returned to the squad, but the coach kept faith with Terry as captain of the side. Wilkinson said, 'He's a natural leader and he gives us a presence. He has had a struggle at Chelsea but he has never allowed it to stop him fighting for a place.' England beat Mexico 3–0 in a comfortable victory at Filbert Street, but Terry was one of six players replaced at half-time as Wilkinson made the mass substitutions now so common in international friendlies.

The game in Athens 12 days later was an entirely different affair, however, as Terry and his team-mates came up against a talented Greece. The young Lions were totally outplayed in the first half and went 2–0 down. After the interval things got even worse. With an hour gone, Terry nodded a long ball back toward Stephen Bywater, only for the ball to squirm under the West Ham keeper's body. Terry was credited with the own goal but it was clear where the blame lay. The England players began to lose their cool at 3–0, and three of them were quickly booked for petulance and cynical fouls.

Carrick pulled a goal back after 85 minutes, with a fine drive from outside the area, but Luke Young was sent off minutes later for retaliating to a smack in the face, which was unseen by the referee. The Young incident sparked a 20-man brawl. Soon after, Terry followed his team-mate off the pitch for an early bath. With his heart still racing after the mêlée, the Chelsea defender launched himself at Dimitris Salpigidis. Terry claims he got the ball, but it was a dreadful two-footed lunge and the Greek player was fortunate to escape serious injury as he was scythed to the ground.

It was an uncharacteristic rush of blood to the head, but it couldn't overshadow a memorable few months for the youngster. His fine form in the second half of the campaign had helped the Blues move up from 14th to finish sixth in the table, and he was named Chelsea's Player of the Season. 'It's unbelievable to be voted player of the year when you consider the squad at this club,' Terry said. 'It's a great honour.'

6

John Terry told the *News of the World*, 'I'm not going to sit on the bench for two or three years just watching people play in my position. That would be a step back for me. I want to play Premiership football week in, week out. I played 23 games last season in Chelsea's first team and I need to keep improving.' But now he was understandably upset. After a fantastic breakthrough season in Ranieri's team, he was expecting to start the season as part of the first-choice defence. But the 2001-02 season was going to one of the hardest in the defender's career, if not on the pitch then certainly off it.

Following Frank Leboeuf's departure for Marseille, the English youngster wanted to form a new partnership with the Ghana-born colossus Marcel Desailly. But the Italian manager needed another centre-back following the departure of Leboeuf and Jes Hogh, so he signed William Gallas to bolster his squad. 'I have been reading about him in the papers,' said Terry. 'The fact that he is a central defender and he said he was looking forward to playing alongside Marcel Desailly has given me food for thought. I'm not sure what's going to happen next season. Will the manager play the new signing with Marcel or me? I just don't know. I'll now have to go back and prove to the manager again that I should be first choice.'

With quotes like these coming from the England Under-21 international, the sharks began to circle. Sensing possible unhappiness in a great young player, Steve McClaren tried to lure Terry away from Chelsea to Middlesbrough. Plenty of other clubs were also in the hunt. But Ranieri wasn't interested in selling his young star; he was merely transforming the squad he had inherited less than a year before and strengthening where necessary. The other new arrivals were the former Arsenal midfielder Emmanuel Petit and Dutch winger Boudewijn Zenden, both from Barcelona, but much more important for the future of Chelsea was the signing of Frank Lampard from West Ham. The young England midfielder crossed London for £11m and was determined to make his mark for club and country.

With the signing of Lampard and the continuing development of Terry, Chelsea had two players who could form a world-class English spine to the team for years to come. Desailly was appointed as the new Chelsea captain following the departure of Wise, and Terry started the season alongside his new skipper in the middle of the Blues defence. Chelsea got the campaign off to a bright start with home draws against tough opposition in Newcastle United and Arsenal. They quickly banished the previous season's dismal away record with a win against Southampton on the South Coast.

Then Howard Wilkinson was sacked following England u-21s' miserable display in Athens. His replacement was David Platt, who had seen enough of Terry during his brief loan spell at Nottingham Forest to confirm him as skipper of the side. Terry and all his young team-mates were delighted with the new coach. 'The lads respect him so much. His training is first class,' the Chelsea man said. Terry was now harbouring serious ambitions of forcing his way into the full squad. His performances on the field indicated that the wait wouldn't be too long, but his off-field misbehaviour would lead to a substantial delay in achieving his England dream.

On 11 September 2001, 19 men affiliated with Osama bin Laden and Al-Qaeda simultaneously hijacked four United States domestic commercial airliners, two of which were crashed into the Twin Towers of the World Trade Centre in New York, causing the buildings to collapse. The third aircraft crashed into the Pentagon, home to the US Department of Defence, and the fourth plane, apparently heading towards either Capitol Hill or the White House in Washington DC, crashed into a field in Pennsylvania, following passenger resistance. The official records count 2,986 men, women and children dead after the largest suicide assault in the history of the world.

One of the immediate effects of the atrocities was the grounding of aircraft across the globe, leaving holidaymakers stuck at airports and, as far as the Chelsea players were concerned, the postponement of their UEFA Cup first-round, first-leg tie against Levski Sofia at Stamford Bridge. Once training was finished, a lot of the players went for lunch together and, with no match now until Sunday, the beer inevitably began to flow. A couple of drinks turned into an alcohol-fuelled rampage and Terry was part of the group that behaved disgracefully in the Heathrow airport area, shocking and distressing members of the public, many of whom were already traumatised, wondering if their families were caught up in the terror attack. When the story hit the papers, the nation was outraged. Chelsea managing director Colin Hutchinson denounced the players' behaviour and imposed the maximum fine of a fortnight's wages on each. Terry issued a regretful statement but it would be a long time before his reputation was restored.

Back on the pitch, things were going from strength to strength for Terry and his team-mates. In the second leg of their UEFA Cup tie, the imposing centre-back registered his first European goal, forcing the ball over the line in Sofia after Desailly had nodded down a Petit corner. That goal killed off the tie after a 3–0 win in London the week before, and Chelsea eventually went through as 5–0 aggregate winners.

Things got a bit trickier for the Blues in the second round when they were paired with Hapoel Tel-Aviv. The then-political climate meant there were obvious security concerns about a trip to Israel. In the wake of the terrorist attacks on 11 September and America's missile attacks on Afghanistan, a number of players were reluctant to travel for the away leg and, after consulting with the manager, William Gallas, Manu Petit, Graeme Le Saux, Albert Ferrer, Eidur Gudjohnsen and Marcel Desailly decided to stay at home.

Terry had no qualms about travelling. 'I was always

convinced it would be safe,' the centre-back said. 'Once we're out there, warming up for the game, it will all go out of our minds. We'll focus the same way we do before every other match. The UEFA Cup is a big competition for us. We went out in the first round last year and we must focus on getting a good result to take back to London. We have a big enough squad to cope in every position, and it's a great chance for some of the youngsters who have come out here with us.'

With so many Chelsea players choosing to stay at home, it was always likely to be a tough day at the office for the Blues. Mario Melchiot didn't help matters by getting himself sent off early in the second half for kicking out at an opponent, with the home side firmly in control. Fortunately for Chelsea, keeper Mark Bosnich was in inspired form on his debut and he made a number of spectacular saves to keep his team in the game. After 89 minutes, it looked like the Blues would take a 0–0 draw back to England. But as the clock ticked down, the home side bagged two late goals to get a well-deserved win. The first came when Terry handled a cross and Shimon Gershon scored the penalty. While Chelsea were still reeling from this setback, Sergei Klaschenco headed home a cross.

The Blues were adamant that the first loss of the season wouldn't affect their league form and came out fighting in their next game at Elland Road. Against a high-flying Leeds side, Terry and his team-mates battled to a 0–0 draw and the Essex youngster was impressed with the spirit and desire of the squad. 'The lads were so fired up before the game,' he told the *Daily Mirror*. 'I have never seen anything like it. We need to be like that before every game to be at our best and achieve what we want. That was our best performance of the season without a shadow of doubt and it goes to show what we can do when we are up for it. Everyone has talked about how well we played. Now we need to take things on and show that sort of commitment every week.'

Chelsea slumped to a first league defeat of the season, losing 2–1 to West Ham after a lethargic display. 'We cannot use tiredness and the number of games as an excuse for our performance at West Ham,' Terry said. 'Sometimes we have to play two or three games in a week as professional footballers. There's no doubt we are fit enough and we have a big enough squad to cope, so we can't blame that.'

Chelsea were stuttering and, four days later, they drew with Derby County, their fourth away game in 10 days, but the next game up was the home leg against Hapoel Tel-Aviv and Terry was desperate to turn the tie around. He was extra-motivated to keep a clean sheet and try to beat the Israeli side, because an extended UEFA Cup run would certainly benefit his chances of making it into the full England squad. Other players had caught the eye of Sven-Goran Eriksson in matches against the continent's finest, and Terry was keen to push his claim. Unfortunately for Terry and Chelsea, Hapoel proved their first-leg heroics were no fluke and secured a 1–1 draw at the Bridge. The Blues enjoyed the majority of possession, but failed to turn chances into goals and their European football was finished for another season.

Terry still had the chance to play on the continent,

though, as England's Young Lions faced Holland in the UEFA Under-21 Championship play-off match. The first leg was in Utrecht and Platt's side showed great quality to fight back from 2–0 down to draw 2–2. Due to his suspension following the Greece game, Terry had missed some matches and, with vice-captain Dunn out injured, Aston Villa's Gareth Barry had taken over the captaincy. But with Dunn and the Chelsea man both available again, it was the Blackburn midfielder who was skipper now.

The second leg was played a week later in Derby, and the England Under-21 defence had to be on top form to guarantee the team's progress to the European Championship finals. Terry and Ledley King were at their best in front of Chris Kirkland, and the young Coventry keeper was exceptional as the home side secured a 1–0 win to take them to the championship in Switzerland.

Since losing to Hapoel Tel-Aviv in the UEFA Cup, Chelsea had struggled to beat anybody. Ranieri's side drew five and lost one of their next seven matches and things grew worse for the Blues as a 0–0 home draw with Blackburn Rovers ended with boos and jeers from the Stamford Bridge crowd. The fans were losing patience. The pressure on Ranieri was mounting but a 2–0 win over Leeds United in the League Cup helped to alleviate some of the anxiety over the manager's position, and the players were in no mood to see him leave. 'I would love to see him remain here and the other lads feel the same,' Terry told a press conference.

'The coach has given me my chance and I owe him a lot. Claudio has been fine about everything and told us earlier this week that he was right behind the players.' The players would need to show their backing for the manager for their next match, away at Old Trafford.

7

Alex Ferguson's side hadn't enjoyed the best autumn but were still expected to beat the Blues at home. The match brought Terry up against Ruud van Nistelrooy for the first time, and his team-mates warned him about the Dutch danger man.

'The day before a game, I look at the striker I am playing against,' Terry told the *Daily Telegraph*. 'Van Nistelrooy's all-round game is superb. Mario Melchiot and Jimmy Floyd Hasselbaink know him from Holland, and they were saying before we played United that his touch was unbelievable. I was thinking: "His touch can't be as good as Juan Sebastian Veron's or David Beckham's." But there were a couple of moments when I felt I could get the ball and he would take it away and I was thinking: "Yeah, Mario and Jimmy were right."'

Terry had a lot of respect for his opposition, but Chelsea put one over on the Red Devils winning 3–0. It was the fifth league defeat inflicted on Ferguson's side and it wasn't even Christmas. The champions had little chance of defending their title after such a poor first half of the season but a win at the 'Theatre of Dreams' gave the Blues' aspirations a big boost.

It wasn't just the team performance that had the critics purring. Terry continued to put in mature and commanding displays at the heart of the Blues' defence. With Desailly out injured, the England defender took more responsibility alongside Gallas and, as the pair formed an excellent partnership, there was more talk of Terry moving up into the full England squad in time for the World Cup finals. The young defender's fine form meant that other rewards soon came his way. Against Charlton Athletic at Stamford Bridge on 5 December 2001, John Terry led out Chelsea for the very first time as captain.

'Claudio came to me the day before the game,' Terry told Chelsea TV, 'and it was a big surprise because at the time Graeme Le Saux was second in line, and there were obviously other players ahead of me, but Claudio said I had come on as a player and I was ready for that role. He said: "This is the game I am going to give it to you," and I remember Graeme coming up to me and wishing me good luck and saying how I was the future of the club and it was all about me. The manager and the players thought I was the right choice. Everyone was backing me, from Jimmy to Gianfranco, and when you have players like that supporting you then you can't go wrong.'

Unfortunately for Terry, there could still be disappointments even with those brilliant players behind him. His first game as captain ended in defeat with a header from Kevin Lisbie bringing Chelsea's unbeaten home record to an end.

As much as Terry tried to keep his feet on the ground

and play down any suggestions of World Cup glory, the press were hell-bent on pushing the Chelsea youngster into the squad to face Argentina, Sweden and Nigeria in Group F of the summer's tournament in Japan and Korea. The media quizzed the men who matter and the replies were unrelentingly excellent. David Platt was not alone in his upbeat assessment: 'Physically tough, mentally strong, reads the game well and not fazed by either the cleverest or the quickest striker,' the England Under-21 coach said.

Terry knew all he could do was keep playing as well as he could but he was concerned with Chelsea's up-and-down season. 'The main frustration at the moment is our own irritating inconsistency,' he said. 'Last season we struggled to win away from home, and this time we're struggling to win at Stamford Bridge. We don't seem to be able to put our finger on what's wrong.' At least Ranieri could be sure there was nothing wrong in defense. In fact he had an embarrassment of riches with Desailly on his way back from injury, and Terry and Gallas conceding only one goal in eight games.

In the run-up to Christmas the attack started to fire as well. The Blues beat Liverpool 4–0 and Bolton 5–1 in two dominant displays at the Bridge. They came down to earth with a 2–1 defeat at Arsenal on Boxing Day but, even then, the Gunners' boss Arsène Wenger had complimentary things to say about the Blues' defence: 'I think Terry is outstanding. He and Gallas did well against us on Boxing Day. We had to work very hard to create chances. Chelsea went to Leeds and did not concede a goal, did the same at Manchester United and the same against Liverpool. That's not coincidence. It shows the two boys have great qualities.'

Chelsea were sixth in the table and Terry had started all 27 matches so far in the campaign, even leading the Blues out on occasion. He was also captain of the England Under-21s, and was tipped by some pundits to make the step up to the senior side sooner rather than later. But away from the pitch Terry had embarrassed himself in the wake of 11 September and, as he entered the New Year, it became clear that as difficult as the fall-out from that episode had been for the Essex lad, it was nothing compared to what lay around the corner.

On the evening of Thursday, 3 January 2002, Terry went out with Jody Morris and Des Byrne to celebrate the birth of Morris's daughter. After a meal Terry drove the three of them from Epsom into London They headed to the Wellington Club, a place that is very popular with London's rich and famous. The trio drank heavily and, after a while, the staff deemed that they had outstayed their welcome. Soon the doormen were helping them out of the club and as they left, a fight broke out.

The police arrived to find the entrance littered with blood and broken glass and arrested Terry and Byrne. Later Morris was also arrested. The newspapers were soon aware that the England Under-21 captain had been out drinking just 36 hours before an important FA Cup tie. Later, Terry was charged with assault, causing actual bodily harm and affray. The prosecution then added wounding with intent to cause grievous bodily harm and having a bottle as an offensive weapon. The wounding charge carried a life sentence as its maximum penalty.

Coming in the wake of the drunken binge at Heathrow less than four months previously, people at Chelsea and in the football world at large had genuine grounds for concern. Just how much did the youngster want to play professional football? Certainly his international career was immediately put on hold. England manager Sven-Goran Eriksson announced, under pressure from his bosses at the FA, that no player facing legal action would be considered for selection until their case was resolved.

Chelsea fined him two weeks' wages but continued to play him, and Terry and Morris both started in the League Cup semi-final first-leg against Spurs on the same day as their first court appearance. Chelsea beat their London rivals 2–1 at Stamford Bridge after their two starlets entered pleas of not guilty in the morning. The next court date was set for mid-February.

With their continued presence in both domestic cup competitions, Chelsea had nine matches in January. With Desailly fit again, Ranieri took the opportunity to rest Terry for an FA Cup replay against Norwich, and he wasn't missed as the Blues won 4–0. He returned refreshed for the next game as Chelsea hammered West Ham 5–1 at Stamford Bridge, but there was a far less accomplished performance in the following match at White Hart Lane. The second leg of the semi-final was a disaster for the Blues and they threw away a 2–1 lead from the first leg and were knocked out of the cup after a second-half capitulation. Terry made an uncharacteristic error for Spurs' first goal, the first sign that his off-field problems might be interfering with his performances on the pitch.

But whatever the reason for Terry's mistake, it wasn't enough to dent the confidence of the manager and Ranieri continued to pick the youngster in the Chelsea back-line.

Terry's form soon picked up and, after helping his side shut out Leeds on the way to a 2–0 win in west London, he was again making headlines for the right reasons. Chelsea dug in deep to beat Leicester, twice coming from behind to win 3–2 in the last minute, and they repeated the trick four days later to beat West Ham in the FA Cup fourth-round replay at Upton Park. Terry's goal in the 93rd minute stopped the tie going to extra-time and put the Blues through to the next round.

Claudio Ranieri was very happy for his troubled star and declared: 'John Terry is a strong character and a strong man. He was down after the Leicester game on Saturday, when he allowed James Scowcroft to score twice. So his winner was a very important goal both for his confidence and the club.'

This was followed by rumours that England might lift their ban on Terry for the World Cup but, before any conclusion could be reached, the Chelsea stopper fractured a toe in his right foot against Aston Villa, which put him out of action for the foreseeable future. The injury brought to an end his run of 35 consecutive Premiership starts.

While Terry's maturity on the field belied his tender years, his off-field antics were occasionally in stark contrast both crass and immature. He again found himself in the news for all the wrong reasons when he was accused of disgusting behaviour in another nightclub. His bad behaviour was putting his career at risk, especially as Chelsea were doing very well without him. In the FA Cup fifth round they came from 1–0 down to beat Preston 3–1, and followed that up by winning three out of four London derbies in the space of 11 days, the most impressive of which was an FA Cup quarter-final win at White Hart Lane.

Terry returned to the Chelsea team over the Easter weekend and marked his comeback with a goal in the 2–1 win over Derby. He replaced the injured Gallas at half-time and opened the scoring five minutes later, heading home a left-wing cross from close range. The win ensured three more valuable points to help the Blues' quest for fourth place in the league, which would also serve as a ticket into the Champions League. A win against Everton the following weekend helped was a big boost, but Terry missed most of the match after coming off second best in a collision with one of the goalposts. The big defender needed 12 stitches to close the wound.

The fact that the court case wouldn't start until the summer ended Terry's hopes of making the World Cup squad, and he wouldn't even be able to play for the Under-21 side that he had led to the European Championship finals. 'I am really gutted,' he said in the *Sun*. 'Not just about not being in the senior squad but I have been a major part of the Under-21 side. I am so disappointed about not being allowed to go there.' Terry quickly put his personal disappointment behind him, however, as he helped Chelsea edge past Fulham into the FA Cup Final.

On the evening after the semi-final, Terry attended the PFA dinner as one of the six contenders for the Young Player of the Year Award. Nominated by his fellow players, he was up against Steven Gerrard, Ledley King, Michael Ricketts, Darius Vassell and Craig Bellamy. The Welsh striker, Bellamy, walked away with the trophy but Terry was glad to know that the other players still held him in such high regard.

Having missed the starting line-up for only 10 games in the season – nine while out injured and one due to his arrest – Terry was confident of starting the match at the Millennium Stadium where he would have to face Thierry Henry. In an interview he revealed his superstition: 'Every night before we play, I give the 2000 medal a kiss for good luck. I always look at it and think of that day; my best memory is definitely being part of that FA Cup winning team.'

As an unused substitute at the 2000 FA Cup Final, Terry had already had a taste of the atmosphere and intensity of the big occasion but now he was looking forward to playing. Unluckily for the young defender, some more bad luck off the pitch conspired to prevent him from starting. 'I had a virus in the morning. It affected my ears and I lost my balance,' he said. 'I woke up dizzy, staggered into a chair and phoned the doctor. That was at 7am. But I was disappointed I didn't start the match. I had an injection to clear the virus, then a fitness test and said I was 100 per cent but the manager decided not to go with me. It was five minutes before I was going down to the team meeting and I heard a knock on the door and I knew straight away it was the manager. I opened the door and he told me I wasn't in the starting line-up. After he'd gone, I felt like crying. It would have been a great achievement to start in the FA Cup Final but it wasn't to be. He just said to me that, with what had happened, he wasn't going to play me.'

But Terry did get onto the pitch when he replaced Babayaro at half-time. The reshuffled Blues found their feet quickly after the break and Arsenal were soon on the back foot, but when the first goal came in the 69th minute it was the Gunners who took the lead against the run of play. Ray Parlour's stunning shot into the top corner from 25 yards galvanised Arsène Wenger's team and, 10 minutes later, they were 2–0 up after an even more impressive strike from Freddie Ljungberg. Terry was left with an FA Cup runners-up medal to go with his winners' medal from two years previously, but the season wasn't yet finished because the FA had moved this final forward a week to allow more preparation time for the World Cup.

Next up was the final league game of the season at home to Aston Villa. Chelsea had already secured their UEFA Cup spot and were unable to overhaul Newcastle to claim a Champions League berth, and Villa were merely fighting for eighth place in the league. Ranieri's players were understandably down after losing the Cup Final and failed to raise themselves for the visit of Villa, losing the game 3–1.

But back to the trial. John Terry, Des Byrne and Jody Morris entered pleas of not guilty. And on Thursday, 22 August 2002, the 14th day of the case, seven-and-a-half months after the incident, John Terry was found not guilty on all four charges. Morris was also cleared. Byrne was found guilty only of possessing an offensive weapon, fined £2,000 and ordered to pay costs of £1,000.

Terry was delighted and his solicitor Steven Barker made a statement outside the court: 'Anyone who saw him give evidence in that witness box will have no doubt of the enormous stress and strain John has been under for the last eight months because of some monstrous allegations that he took a bottle to a bouncer. He is extremely relieved and pleased at this verdict. His words were that justice has been done. He wants to thank his legal team, Chelsea Football Club and, last but not least, his family and friends.'

8

Less than a year after his trial, John Terry at last won his first England cap. 'I waited a long time to get my England debut but, when it finally came, I was the proudest man ever,' he said. It rounded off another memorable season that had started badly for Terry who was suffering with a knee injury that required an operation.

Once fit, he again had to force his way past two Frenchmen to get into the Chelsea team since Marcel Desailly and William Gallas had developed their own excellent partnership in the Blues defence. Ranieri's side began the season in impressive form and were unbeaten after six games, including draws against Arsenal and Manchester United. But Terry's recovery from knee surgery took longer than expected, with further complications including the dizzy spells he suffered before the FA Cup Final.

After his lengthy absence, Terry took to the field for his first match of the season away to Viking Stavanger in the UEFA Cup. Chelsea travelled to Norway with a 2–1 lead from the first leg, but the last-minute goal they conceded at the Bridge would come back to haunt them as they lost 4–2 on the night, and 5–4 on aggregate, to crash out in the early stages of European competition for the third year in a row.

Terry was struggling after his absence and was dropped to the reserves in search of some much-needed match sharpness. Immediately the tabloid papers started to link him with a move to Arsenal, Liverpool or Newcastle but he only had eyes for the Blues. Gallas and Desailly performed admirably in Terry's place, and the he had to make do with substitute appearances as the two Frenchmen kept clean sheets in five consecutive league matches. Barring the odd 10 or 15 minutes in the Premiership, Terry's only chance to impress came in the League Cup. In the third-round tie against Gillingham, he showed he had fully recovered from his injury problems as he and Gallas stifled the Gills attack again and again to put Chelsea's name into the hat for the next round.

Terry again deputised for Desailly in defence and as captain when Everton came to the Bridge in the fourth round, and the Blues dominated from start to finish to win the game 4–1. Ranieri still had plenty of faith in him but was loath to change a winning formula, so Terry was back on the bench for the trip to Goodison Park on his birthday. Chelsea beat Everton 3–1, the three points lifting them to second in the table. The young defender's long wait for a Premiership start came when Desailly missed the game against Middlesbrough for personal reasons. In the Frenchman's absence, Terry was once again made captain. Victory against Boro would take Chelsea to the top of the table for the first time in three years but they could only draw 1–1, with Terry grabbing the equaliser.

With Desailly still missing, Terry led the side out against Manchester United in the League Cup quarter-final, but neither he nor Gallas could stop Diego Forlan from hitting the only goal of the game, 10 minutes from time, to put Chelsea out of the cup. In fact they were out of two knock-out competitions before Christmas, but this failed to upset the Blues' good league form and they won the next match 2–0 against Aston Villa, extending their unbeaten run in the Premiership to 10 games. Desailly returned for the next match to reclaim the armband but Terry retained his place in the team for the goalless draw against Southampton. However he was back on the bench for the next two matches as the Blues' unbeaten streak came to a spectacular end with defeats at Leeds and Arsenal. That brought Terry back into the side for the FA Cup third-round tie against Middlesbrough, which they won 1–0 despite having Cudicini sent off.

His hopes of an extended run were thwarted in the next match against Charlton, when he fell awkwardly on a very sandy surface at the Bridge and had to be replaced after 16 minutes. The new injury meant he missed the trip to Old Trafford and a defeat that saw Chelsea fall to fourth in the table. Fortunately it was the only game he missed, and he was fit enough to replace the suspended Desailly against Shrewsbury Town in the FA Cup fourth round when he led his side to a comfortable 4–0 win. That proved a turning point for Terry as he put his injury troubles behind him and went on to start the next 15 matches.

Terry scored in a 2–2 FA Cup match with Arsenal and

again when they swept Manchester City away 5–0. His good form since returning to the first team had not gone unnoticed, and the Chelsea defender received his first England call-up for the Euro 2004 qualification matches against Liechtenstein and Turkey. Sven-Goran Eriksson was without Sol Campbell and Wes Brown for the vital games, and he liked what he saw in the Chelsea man: 'He is a good defender and is improving his passing as well. Someone told me he wants to be captain of Chelsea and England. They are good ambitions,' the Swede said.

But before Terry could join up with his new England colleagues, there was the considerable obstacle of Thierry Henry's Arsenal and an FA Cup quarter-final replay. It would be a tough assignment but the Chelsea manager had no doubts about his young defender's ability to handle arguably the world's finest attacker. 'When I was in Italy I said I had seen the Muhammad Ali of football, because Henry could float like a butterfly and sting like a bee,' Ranieri told the *Daily Express*. 'But Terry is like a man from Mars. I have never seen a centre-forward dominate him, not even Henry.'

Terry was ready for the fight and celebrated his England selection by continuing his rich vein of scoring with two goals against Wenger's team, except the first was an own goal. Midway through the first half, Arsenal broke quickly from defence and Terry, running back towards his own area under pressure from Francis Jeffers and Sylvain Wiltord, turned Patrick Vieira's cross past Cudicini. Things got worse for the Blues when they went two down before the break, but in the 66th minute Pascal Cygan was sent off for hauling Hasselbaink to the ground and Terry made amends for his own goal with a fine header past Stuart Taylor with 11 minutes left. But all hopes of a Chelsea revival were dashed soon afterwards as Lauren scored a rare goal to make it 3–1.

Terry suffered another disappointment when wasn't involved in either of the two England matches with Eriksson who put Rio Ferdinand, Gareth Southgate, Sol Campbell and Jonathan Woodgate ahead of him. But the Chelsea defender gained valuable experience training with such quality players and put that into practice back at Chelsea. With only the league left to concentrate on, the players channelled their disappointment into claiming that last Champions League spot which had proved so elusive in recent years. They beat Sunderland and Bolton to narrow the gap with Newcastle to just one point, and keep their European destiny firmly in their own hands. But Chelsea faltered on their way to the finishing line, drawing at home to Fulham and losing away games against West Ham and Aston Villa, despite Terry scoring his sixth goal of the season at Villa Park.

They still had qualification within reach though as they faced Liverpool on the final day of the season. The two sides were level on 64 points after 37 games and knew that whoever won the game would take fourth place in the league along with the final Champions League spot. The loser would be heading for the UEFA Cup. Chelsea had a superior goal difference and only needed a point in front of a sell-out Stamford Bridge. The Blues were also in desperate need of the money that the Champions League would generate since there was talk of Ranieri having to sell some of his best assets, including Gallas, Hasselbaink and even Terry, so it was a great relief when they did qualify with a 2–1 win over the Reds. First-half goals from Desailly and Gronkjaer gave Chelsea the points after Sami Hyypia's opener.

Terry missed the big clash due to a thigh injury but he was fit to join the England squad for their end-of-season matches. Once again he was left out of the game, against South Africa in Durban, but he was on the bench for the next friendly a week-and-a-half later and he came on at the interval to make his full England debut. At Leicester's Walkers Stadium on Tuesday, 3 June 2003, John Terry replaced Gareth Southgate at half-time to come on for the second 45 minutes of England's friendly with Serbia & Montenegro. The score was 1–1 when the Chelsea defender entered the fray. He played alongside Matthew Upson in the middle of the back four and helped keep the Serbs at bay. West Ham's Joe Cole hit a brilliant free-kick eight minutes from time to win the match.

It was time for the Chelsea defender to take stock. He desperately wanted to stay at Stamford Bridge but was concerned at the way the club was treating him: 'It's a little bit frustrating when Chelsea's future is looking good and things aren't being sorted out. You see players at other clubs being rewarded for doing well. I don't feel as if I've been rewarded for what I've done over the last few seasons. I've had the same deal for two years and, if things can't be resolved, I'm going to have to start thinking about my own future. I don't want to be up there with the likes of Jimmy and Marcel. I just want to be on a nice level.'

Terry had certainly proved his worth to the Blues in a season blighted by injury; he only started 25 games but

still managed to score six goals. All the people in charge of the club appreciated what a gifted young player they had on their hands. They wanted to keep him at the Bridge and a new investor meant that money would no longer be an issue. Chelsea were about to become the richest club in the world.

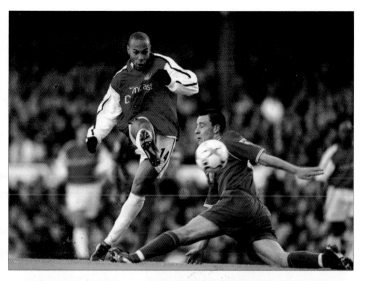

Above: Few strikers find success easy against John Terry, but he has always had a healthy respect for Arsenal frontman Thierry Henry, here firing a shot past his marker in January 2001.

Below: Defenders also score goals! Later in the same game, Terry celebrates scoring the equaliser.

John Terry secured his senior debut for England against Serbia Montenegro in June 2003, days after more tabloid speculation about his off-pitch antics.

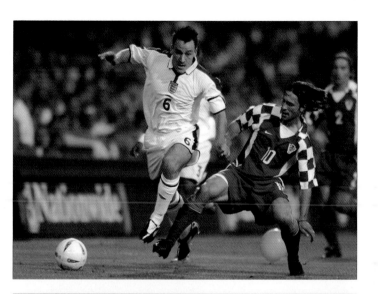

Another match against an unpredictable and talented Balkans team – this time a friendly against Croatia at Portman Road in August 2003. Here, Terry displays his agility and presence on the ball in a game which earned him well-deserved praise.

Above: Watched by manager Claudio Ranieri, Chelsea's Jimmy Floyd Hasselbaink and John Terry exercise in training, November 2003.

Below: John Terry looks on as Ranieri answers questions about his future in May 2004. Terry saw the Italian coach as the man who gave him his first chance.

John Terry lifts the Carling Cup, the club's first trophy under Jose Mourinho, following a hard-fought 3–2 victory over Liverpool in February 2005.

Above: John Terry jumps to score a valuable winning goal against Catalan giants Barcelona in the Champions League, March 2005. Chelsea won 5–4 on aggregate, and they were into the last eight.

Below: 2005 was not an unmitigated success for Terry. Here he battles for the ball against Denmark during a friendly in August which gave England their worst defeat since 1980, when they lost 4–1.

Another award – and this time it's personal. John Terry holds the
PFA Players' Player of the Year trophy in April 2005.

Above: Déjà vu? John Terry celebrates winning back-to-back Premiership titles with team mates Frank Lampard and Eidur Gudjohnsen (now of Tottenham Hotspur).

Below left: End of the world… A tearful Terry rues England's exit from the 2006 World Cup in Germany.

Below right: England's former captain wore the armband with pride against Greece at Old Trafford. He scored the first goal in the 4–0 victory, his first full game as captain.

9

John Terry suddenly found himself surrounded by new faces. By early September Claudio Ranieri had made 12 signings (getting rid of seven players), and Chelsea were transformed from the paupers of recent seasons into Europe's biggest spenders. It really was a new squad for a new Chelsea. The reason for the change was Roman Arkadievich Abramovich.

The new owner was more than three months younger than Gianfranco Zola but worth several billion pounds. He had obtained his vast fortune by acquiring shares cheaply in freshly privatised companies following the fall of Soviet communism and, in early July 2003, Abramovich became the majority shareholder of Chelsea Village holding company, making him the owner of the Blues and simultaneously rendering the club debt of approximately £80m inconsequential. His first priority was to secure the existing assets, which meant tying down Chelsea's best players to new contracts. Terry was at the head of the queue. After eight months of on-and-off, back-and-forth negotiations, he signed a new four-year deal worth £50,000 a week. It was a staggering pay rise and showed how valuable the young defender was in the eyes of his employers. Terry was delighted.

New players were arriving thick and fast. The first two men to join Abramovich's Chelsea were the goalkeepers Jurgen Macho and Marco Ambrosio, whose deals had been negotiated under the 'old' Chelsea regime. However, they would soon be forgotten under the avalanche of money that brought in so many fresh faces. Glen Johnson was signed from West Ham on a £6m deal that was meant to be £3m up front with a further £3m depending on appearances, but the day after the transfer the whole £6m arrived in the Hammers' coffers. Wayne Bridge was next, a second young English full-back, this time from Southampton for £7m. Having strengthened the defence, Ranieri turned his attentions to midfield and signed Geremi for £7m from Real Madrid, although he had spent the previous season at Middlesbrough, as well as Blackburn's exciting Irish winger Damien Duff for a massive £17m.

Terry was sad to see Stamford Bridge's favourite Italian, Gianfranco Zola, depart. The talented midfielder had been out of contract at the end of the previous season and, with the then cash-strapped club unable to offer him a realistic new deal, the little genius had negotiated a return to his native Sardinia to play for Cagliari. A man of pride and honour, Zola had given his word to the Italian club and, even though he had signed no contract, he stuck by his promise and returned home despite a fantastic last-minute bid from Chelsea who were now funded by Abramovich. 'I think I have made the right decision,' Zola said. 'My reputation with the Sardinian people was at stake.'

Before the season began, the future of another Italian was also thrown into doubt as the pressure mounted on Ranieri. The world's best coaches were being linked increasingly with the Blues but it didn't make much sense to let one manager sign so many players if he was going to be replaced before the season kicked off, which meant Ranieri just got on with his job. Pre-season matches included the Premier League Asia Cup, when Chelsea beat the Malaysian national team 4–1 and defeated Newcastle United 4–3 on penalties after the game finished 0–0 after 90 minutes. The spot-kicks went to sudden death and it was Terry who held his nerve to win the final, making him the captain who lifted the first Chelsea trophy of the new era.

Ranieri's options increased further as Juan Sebastian Veron and Joe Cole joined to give the Blues that something extra in the final third, and the Romanian striker Adrian Mutu signed from Parma to provide competition for Hasselbaink and Gudjohnsen up front. The squad was still far from complete, though, and Ranieri splashed some more cash bringing in Argentinian striker Hernan Crespo from Inter Milan, Real Madrid's French midfielder Claude Makelele and Alexei Smertin from Bordeaux, although the Russian went straight out on a season-long loan to Portsmouth. Throughout the spending spree, several centre-backs were linked with the club, but despite all the millions at his disposal, Ranieri kept faith with Terry, Desailly, Gallas and the young, improving Robert Huth. Terry was back at the top of that list and would start almost every game.

The players were good enough to play Champions

League football, which they secured by beating MSK Zilina 5–0 on aggregate in a qualifying round before being drawn in Group G to face Sparta Prague, Besiktas and Lazio. The league campaign also started well, and Chelsea won six of their first seven Premiership matches, drawing the other 2–2 with Blackburn.

Terry's season had started brilliantly at Chelsea, and he was once again involved with England as they attempted to secure their passage to Euro 2004. To his delight, the young centre-back was involved in every game for his country throughout autumn. The friendly against Croatia at Portman Road on 20 August was Terry's first start for England, and he took his club form forward with a display as confident and composed as anyone could have wished. He was the only man to play the whole match and was even handed the captain's armband for the final 10 minutes. England won game 3–1, making it six wins on the trot, perfect form heading into the vital European Championship qualification matches.

Against Macedonia in Skopje, Terry continued his international development with his first competitive start for England. Playing alongside Sol Campbell in the middle of defence, the Chelsea stalwart proved valuable in the opposition box as well, winning the penalty from which David Beckham hit the winner after 63 minutes. Four days later, Terry helped England make it eight wins in a row as they beat Liechtenstein 2–0, also securing a first clean sheet for his country alongside Birmingham's Matthew Upson. The win over the European minnows meant that a draw in Istanbul would leave England on top of the group and guarantee their place at Euro 2004, while forcing Turkey to take their chances in the play-offs.

Terry was winning only his fifth cap and making just his fourth start for England but his partnership with Campbell was impressive from the first minute to the last. Few onlookers realized that it was only the second time the two had ever played together. For a game of such massive importance, chances kept coming far too easily at both ends, but during the first half all the Turks' efforts came from distance, with Terry and Campbell defending the edge of the box as if their lives depended on it.

England had the perfect opportunity to relieve some of the pressure at the other end when Tugay brought down Steven Gerrard in the area, but as David Beckham ran up to hit the penalty, he slipped and sent the ball sailing over the bar. Yet Terry and Campbell stood firm and the match finished 0–0, sending England to the European Championship finals. The press were unanimous in their praise of Terry after the game: 'KING JOHN' read a headline in the *Sun*; 'RIO WHO?' asked the *Daily Mirror*.

Back in the hard graft of the Premiership, Chelsea had the chance to go top with a trip to Birmingham City. Going into their game in hand over the league-leaders Arsenal, they were just one point behind their London rivals with a superior goal difference. Birmingham had started the season well and, with both sides looking a little tired after the international week, the game ended 0–0. But a point was all Chelsea needed to take top spot, much to the satisfaction of the players. 'I hope we can stay where we are,' Terry said. 'We are aiming to keep going and keep progressing.'

The next hurdle Terry and his team-mates had to overcome was Arsenal, as the table's top two came head to head at Highbury. Chelsea had never beaten Arsène Wenger's side during Ranieri's reign. In fact, the last league victory over the Gunners was back in September 1995. To rub salt in the wound, their London rivals had also knocked the Blues out of the FA Cup in each of the previous three seasons.

Chelsea had to contend with some serious bad luck on the day with Terry suffering a hamstring injury during the warm-up. Mario Melchiot took his place alongside Huth in the centre of defence, but a late mistake by Cudicini gave Arsenal a 2–1 win and put them back to the top of the table. It was Chelsea's first league defeat of the season, and, coming two weeks after an unfortunate 2–0 loss in the Champions League to Besiktas, some people suggested the bubble had burst and it would be back to the inconsistent Chelsea of previous seasons. The players responded to the criticism in the best way possible with a defiant performance against Lazio at Stamford Bridge, fighting back from a goal down to win 2–1.

The spirit the players showed against Lazio helped the Blues to embark on a run of seven successive victories in all competitions, including an excellent 4–0 win in the return match against the Roman side in the Stadio Olimpico, as Claudio Ranieri enjoyed an auspicious homecoming. The team was very settled and, although the run of victories came to an end in the Champions League against Sparta Prague, a 0–0 draw extended the sequence of clean sheets to five. Next up were Manchester United when a Lampard penalty was enough to clinch victory and, with Fulham holding Arsenal to a draw at Highbury, a good day got even better. Chelsea's three points took them back to the top of the table at the end of November. Nine days later when they beat Besiktas 2–0 'away' in a neutral venue in Gelsenkirchen, Chelsea also came out on top of Group G of the Champions League.

One of the most dangerous times in football is when everything is going well and Chelsea crashed back down to earth with a 2–1 defeat to Bolton, the winning goal deflecting in off Terry. That was follow by a trip to Aston Villa in the quarter-final of the League Cup where the players just didn't perform, and again they lost 2–1. The games were coming thick and fast and three days later Chelsea beat Fulham 1–0 at Craven Cottage, but they made it three defeats in four matches on Boxing Day when they crashed to a 4–2 loss at The Valley.

Terry equalised after nine minutes with a fine header from Mutu's free-kick, but it was at the other end that the damage was done as the Addicks ran the Blues defence ragged. This festive blip undermined the great progress the team had made in the first half of the season, but Ranieri's men were third in the table, and still very much alive in the Champions League, with the FA Cup to come.

On the international stage, things continued to go well for Terry who felt very much at home in Eriksson's set-up. In mid-December Ferdinand received an eight-month ban after his failure to submit to drug testing and, although he still had an appeal, the chances of him featuring in the England side were slim. Terry's performance in qualifying for the European Championship had been outstanding, and his club manager had no doubts about his ability to deliver on the big stage. 'Terry proved against Turkey what we always knew about him,' Ranieri said.

'And he came back a bigger and stronger player. Now he is getting experience of Champions League football he can only get better.'

Terry had started 26 of Chelsea's 30 games in the first half of the season so the manager decided to give him a rest in the FA Cup third round. The Blues defence wasn't the same without their home-grown centre-back, and they conceded two goals in a draw with Watford at Vicarage Road. Terry returned to the team for the next match, but the poor form continued and Liverpool stole three points from the Bridge with a 1–0 win.

The sudden rush of bad results added fuel to the flames burning under Ranieri, but the wins came back almost as quickly as they had vanished. Chelsea put together a run of six victories and a draw in the next seven games, to go through to the FA Cup fifth round and to get within a point of Manchester United, who were second in the Premiership.

After beating Portsmouth 2–0 at Fratton Park, Chelsea's next two games were against the Gunners, the first in the FA Cup followed by a league match the following Saturday. They were the kind of challenges Terry relished.

10

With the January transfer window open, Roman Abramovich got his cheque book out again to strengthen the squad with the signing of Scott Parker from Charlton. The young English midfielder had impressed in the Blues' defeat at the Valley, and Ranieri thought he would be a valuable addition. But even with their enhanced squad, Chelsea were unable to overcome Arsenal. The Blues lost to their London rivals in the FA Cup for the fourth consecutive season, and lost again in the league six days later when the Gunners came to Stamford Bridge. In both matches Chelsea had taken the lead and, in both matches, Wenger's side had come back to win 2–1.

Arsenal were running away with the title, but Chelsea were still in the fight for second place, which would secure their return to Champions League football. Their next match was in that competition as the Blues endeavoured to put their domestic disappointments behind them with a trip to Germany to play VfB Stuttgart. Having felt that good fortune had deserted them recently, Chelsea had no cause to complain this time, winning the match by a lucky own goal.

The victory was just what Ranieri's men needed to pick them up, and they showed their character in putting together another fine run of results. Manchester City were brushed aside in the league 1–0, before the Blues secured their place in the Champions League quarter-finals with a resolute display against Stuttgart at Stamford Bridge, getting a 0–0 draw. They were through to the knock-out stages and, when the draw was made, Chelsea's name inevitably came out with the only other English team still in the competition, their big rivals Arsenal.

Chelsea had the best possible preparation for the quarter-final first leg with back-to-back Premiership wins, and Terry was at his imperious best putting in gargantuan performances against Bolton and Fulham. But the Gunners were in incredible form and were still on course for the 'Treble' as March came to an end. They sat at the top of the Premiership unbeaten, were in the semi-final of the FA Cup and now faced Terry and his team-mates in the Champions League, having already beaten them three times that season.

Arsenal were slightly ahead after the first leg at Stamford Bridge, their away goal giving them the advantage following the 1–1 draw, but Desailly was suspended for the return match after his late red card. Yet there was nothing to separate the two sides in west London, and that gave Chelsea confidence for the second leg a fortnight later.

The Blues kept the pressure on Arsenal in the league as well, with wins over Wolves by 5–2 and Spurs 1–0. That made it 15 points from five games since the two teams had met in the league. Terry had never played in a team that had beaten Arsenal, and Chelsea hadn't beaten the Gunners in the last 17 attempts and it looked as though history would repeat itself when Jose Antonio Reyes put the visitors ahead in first-half injury-time, but after the break it was all Chelsea.

Frank Lampard equalised when Lehmann failed to clear Makelele's long-range effort and Arsenal were on the ropes. The Blues drove forward searching for the knock-out blow. Ashley Cole made a miraculous goal-line clearance from an effort by Gudjohnsen after 85 minutes, but two minutes later Bridge charged up the left wing to score the most important goal of his career. The former Southampton full-back played a one-two with Gudjohnsen on the edge of the area, and the beautiful return pass from the Icelandic international received the finish it deserved. The ball nestled in the Arsenal net and Chelsea were through to the Champions League semi-finals.

It could have been the ecstasy and relief of finally beating Arsenal, or the thought of facing Monaco in the last four of the Champions League, or conversely the fact that the Gunners bounced back the following Friday to beat Liverpool and shatter any remaining hopes the Blues may have had of catching them in the league. But whatever the explanation, Chelsea went off the boil in the league and picked up only two points from their next three games.

This wasn't ideal form ahead of the biggest game in the club's history. And their semi-final opponents were no mugs. Monaco had beaten the mighty Real Madrid in their quarter-final, overcoming a 4–2 first-leg deficit. Terry and his team-mates faced one of the toughest tests of their life and were soon on the back foot as Monaco went ahead after 15 minutes. That could have seen Chelsea's heads go down but instead the goal seemed to spur them on. They pushed forward and were level six minutes later through Crespo's close-range finish. The equaliser put the Blues in the ascendancy and they dominated the rest of the half. But no further goals came and the sides were locked 1–1 at the break.

In the run-up to the game, Ranieri had found out that Chelsea had held a secret meeting with Jose Mourinho, the talented young Porto manager, and the Italian was desperate to win the match and prove his credentials. He replaced Gronkjaer with Veron and, when the French side were reduced to 10 men with the dismissal of Andreas Zikos , Ranieri went for the jugular. Unfortunately for the Blues his two additional changes, Hasselbaink for Melchiot and Huth for Parker, disrupted the shape and structure of the side. The 10 men of Monaco scored two more goals and, against the odds, won 3–1.

In the second leg at Stamford Bridge, Chelsea went ahead after 22 minutes, Gronkjaer's fine left-footed cross looping over the Monaco keeper and into the top corner. Chelsea continued to push forward, maintaining the high tempo associated with English football and searching for the goal that would put them in the final. As half-time approached, Lampard added the perfect finish to a crisp move involving Melchiot, Gudjohnsen and Bridge and, for the first time in the tie, the Blues were ahead, courtesy of the away-goals rule. But their joy was short-lived as Hugo Ibarra pulled a goal back deep into first-half injury-time.

Seconds away from the chance to regroup and focus on the final 45 minutes that stood between them and the

Champions League Final, Ibarra's finish knocked the stuffing out of Chelsea. They had one chance to score early in the second half, but Monaco scored again with 30 minutes remaining and it was game over.

As the season drew to a close, Terry had no time to mope around since he had to try and lift himself and his team-mates for a trip to Old Trafford. Arsenal had finally confirmed their status as champions a fortnight earlier, and Chelsea needed one point from Manchester United to secure second place in the league. They achieved their goal with another resilient display. Cudicini saved a penalty and the Blues had to play the final 17 minutes of the match with 10 men, but they still held on for a 1–1 draw, thanks to Gronkjaer's first-half opener. Chelsea were the second-best team in the country.

Terry had once again shown great improvement: his seamless transition to a full England international and his maturing performances as Chelsea captain, with Desailly missing more than half the games, proved the fact. He might have scored only three goals, but he had started 51 of Chelsea's 59 games, and his continued excellence was once again recognised when he was nominated as the PFA Young Player of the Year, though the prize went to his new team-mate Scott Parker.

Second place wasn't good enough for Abramovich, and it wasn't unexpected when Ranieri was sacked. A new man would be coming in to spend some of the Russian's roubles, and the man who had put so much trust in Terry was leaving.

The young defender would never forget what the Italian had done for him, and he had shown his appreciation to his mentor earlier in the season with an incredible gesture after the England match in Istanbul. In his book, Ranieri told a story about the time he saw his young protégé with a package at the training ground. It contained Terry's England shirt from the match against Croatia, his first start for his country, mounted in a glittering frame with England emblems at each corner. The Italian said, 'Well done, JT! Look after it always, it's a lovely souvenir. And framed like that, it looks really good.' Then, a couple of days later, Terry returned to the training ground with a gift for Ranieri. The manager wrote: 'Mounted in a frame, just like the one I had admired, was his England shirt from the qualifier against Turkey in Istanbul, with a dedication: "To Claudio. I will never forget the man who gave me my first chance. John Terry."'

11

John Terry travelled to Portugal for the European Championship finals as one of England's 23-man squad. The Chelsea No. 26 was given '5' as his shirt number, reinforcing his position as one of the first-choice centre-backs for the tournament. Only a year before he didn't have a single cap to his name but now he was performing like a seasoned veteran. He had forced his way into the England side during Ferdinand's suspension, and everyone expected him to partner Sol Campbell when the tournament finally got under way with a big clash against the multi-talented French side. But injury struck again in the build up to the tournament and it didn't respond quickly enough for Terry to face France. Ledley King replaced him in the England defence as they went down 2–1, Zinedine Zidane scoring both the French goals in the dying minutes.

But Terry was back in action as England concentrated on qualifying for the quarter-finals by trying to beat Switzerland and Croatia. He looked a little rusty against the Swiss, but he and Campbell kept a clean sheet while at the other end Wayne Rooney stole the show with two goals in a 3–0 win. Croatia went ahead after six minutes in the final group game but Rooney again guided England to victory, netting twice in a 4–1 win. England faced Portugal in the quarter-finals.

Sven-Goran Eriksson picked the same side for the third successive game, and England got off to the perfect start when Michael Owen latched on to a defensive error to open the scoring after three minutes. But the team was seriously weakened with less than half an hour on the clock, when the inspirational Rooney was forced off injured. The talismanic forward had broken a metatarsal in a collision with Jorge Andrade and his tournament was over.

England looked clueless without the teenager and they would soon be following their best player out of the Championship. They lacked shape and structure and seemed unable to retain the ball. The players didn't look interested in adding to their lead and simply invited the opposition to attack. Terry and the rest of the defence were under constant pressure. Along with Neville, Campbell and Cole, the Chelsea defender dealt admirably with everything that was thrown at them, but eventually Portugal found a way through and it was no less than they deserved. After 83 minutes Helder Postiga headed Simao's cross past James and the home crowd went wild.

There was still time for England to push forward, and in the last minute Owen headed Beckham's free-kick against the bar and then Campbell bundled the ball over the line. But the referee Urs Meier saw an apparent push by Terry on Ricardo and ruled the goal out. The game went into

Silver Goal extra-time. After 110 minutes Rui Costa hit an unstoppable drive from outside the box into the top corner of James' net. With only 10 minutes left England had to attack and, five minutes from time, they hit an equaliser. Terry nodded down a Beckham corner and Lampard was on hand to swivel on the edge of the six-yard box and smash the ball home.

Having helped the team level, the boys from the Bridge then stood up to be counted when the tie went to penalties five minutes later. Both men scored from the spot but England were let down by Beckham and Darius Vassell, and they lost the shoot-out 6–5. 'I'm devastated,' Terry said. 'It's a terrible way to go out of the competition, especially when we thought we'd done enough to go through. I thought it was our night but, in the end, we didn't get it.'

After the disappointment with England, Terry needed a boost. It came on the way to a pre-season tournament with Chelsea. 'When we were flying out on the way to America, the new manager pulled me to the back of the plane. I didn't know what he wanted, but he just said to me: "I can see the lads have a lot of respect for you. I want you to be my captain".' The central defender had originally been apprehensive about Chelsea's new boss, Jose Mourinho, but now he was well on his way to becoming one of his biggest fans.

Jose Mario Santos Mourinho Felix arrived in west London fresh from winning the Champions League in May 2004, a miraculous achievement by a club as small as FC Porto, but it was the natural conclusion to two-and-a-half years of spectacular progress for the club. Having served a coaching apprenticeship under Bobby Robson at Sporting Lisbon, Porto and Barcelona in the early 1990s, Mourinho developed into a world-class coach in his own right after taking over at Porto in January 2002.

The first time Terry met his new manager was when the man from Setubal visited the England team hotel in Manchester before the squad headed out to the European Championships. Mourinho sat down with his new players – Terry, Frank Lampard, Joe Cole and Wayne Bridge – and told them what he thought of them and where he was going to take them. He told the young centre-back that he believed he was one of the best defenders in the world, but he hadn't won anything yet. He added that he, Jose Mourinho, was going to change all that. The fact that the coach had gone to the trouble to seek them out impressed the young Chelsea quartet.

A number of players were released as surplus to requirements at Stamford Bridge, so out went Jimmy Floyd Hasselbaink, Manu Petit, Mario Stanic, Jesper Gronkjaer, Boudewijn Zenden, Neil Sullivan, Marco Ambrosio, Mario Melchiot, Winston Bogarde and former club captain Marcel Desailly. And thanks to Roman Abramovich's billions Ranieri had already signed the Czech goalkeeper Petr Cech and Dutch winger Arjen Robben the previous season, while Mourinho now raided his former club for two defenders, Paulo Ferreira and Ricardo Carvalho.

Yet another of Mourinho's countrymen arrived from Benfica. Tiago Mendes strengthened the midfield and PSV Eindhoven's Mateja Kezman and Marseille's Ivory Coast striker Didier Drogba bolstered the attack. The newcomers sent Abramovich's transfer spending past the £200 million mark and, once Alexei Smertin came back from his loan at Portsmouth and Juan Sebastian Veron and Hernan Crespo were loaned out to Inter and AC Milan, the new squad was all set for the season.

Chelsea kicked off their campaign with a mouth-watering home clash against Manchester United, the ideal way to check out their championship credentials. It was the perfect start. They took all three points thanks to an early goal from Eidur Gudjohnsen. The visitors enjoyed the lion's share of possession, but Terry typified his team's resolve with a determined performance alongside Gallas. The Blues followed it up with two more wins and two more clean sheets. Mourinho was building his team from the back and, in their first eight games, they only conceded one goal when James Beattie scored in the first minute when Southampton came to the Bridge. Even then Chelsea came from behind to win 2–1, thanks to a Beattie own goal and a Lampard penalty.

After a fourth straight league win, Terry reported for England duty as the World Cup qualifying campaign got under way but England capitulated in Vienna, throwing away a 2–0 lead to draw 2–2 with Austria. Eriksson's men let another lead slip four days later, against Poland in Chorzow, but they recovered to win 2–1.

Back at Chelsea the clean sheets kept coming nearly every week, but they lost their 100 per cent start to the campaign immediately after the international break when Aston Villa held them to a 0–0 draw. The next match was against Paris Saint Germain in Europe and Terry opened his account for the season, heading Lampard's corner into an empty net after the keeper lost the ball in flight. The

Blues went on to win the game 3–0 but none of the Chelsea players could find a way past Spurs keeper Paul Robinson in the next game.

After two league draws, the Blues got back on track with a 1–0 win at Middlesbrough, and Chelsea's young skipper made it two goals from two Champions League ties against Mourinho's former club Porto. He completed a hat-trick of sorts when he scored a third Champions League goal against CSKA at the Bridge a month later, heading home a Smertin corner.

Before the game against the Russians, Terry again answered his country's call but he knew he had stiff opposition for his place in the starting line-up. Ferdinand was back after his suspension and Sol Campbell returned after injury for the World Cup qualifiers against Wales and Azerbaijan. The pair had been Eriksson's first-choice partnership before Ferdinand's ban, and the coach decided to revert to that pairing, leaving Terry on to the sidelines. The Chelsea defender watched from the bench as England secured two wins to go to the top of the group with 10 points from four games, putting them in pole position for a place in Germany in 2006.

On returning to Chelsea, Terry found his team's great start had once again been disrupted by the international break, and Mourinho experienced defeat for the first time as a Premiership manager, Manchester City winning 1–0 from an Anelka penalty. Terry helped his side recover by scoring that Champions League goal against CSKA Moscow, a win that rejuvenated the Londoners' challenge and they won their next seven games, a sequence which took them into the last 16 of the

Champions League, the last eight of the League Cup and to the top of the Premiership.

Chelsea were going strong on all fronts and, except for the League Cup clash at Upton Park, Terry had played in every minute of every match and was becoming more and more important to the team's cause. His value in financial terms was brought home by a new contract in early November. Even though his existing deal still had more than two years to run, the club were keen to renegotiate and they boosted his salary to £80,000 a week in 2009.

His long-term future at the Bridge was secure, but Terry still wanted to force his way into the England side and he had another opportunity to do that in November. The squad travelled to Spain without Campbell, who was injured again, so Terry lined up alongside Ferdinand. But the only men to impress were wearing red shirts as England were comprehensively outplayed. The international break again caused Chelsea's form to stutter, and Terry returned to club duty in a 2–2 draw against Bolton. It was frustrating but the skipper again led by example and helped the Blues back to form with two goals against Charlton. Chelsea had lost 4–2 at The Valley in the last visit under Ranieri, but Mourinho's team blitzed the home side 4–0.

Chelsea racked up a second successive 4–0 Premiership win, this time against Newcastle United, and then turned their attentions to Arsenal. Five points separated the two teams at the top but, unlike the previous season, it was the Blues who were in pole position. Having finally got a win against the Gunners at the end of the previous season, Terry hoped his team could repeat the trick in north London to stretch their lead at the top to eight points, but that wasn't to be as Thierry Henry stole the show in a 2–2 draw.

Even after Henry's two goals, Chelsea had only conceded eight goals in their first 16 league games and Mourinho was certain of the reason: he had the world's best defender in his team. 'I know Sir Alex would say Rio Ferdinand. I know Carlo Ancelotti will say Alessandro Nesta, but for me it's John Terry,' the manager said. 'Since the first minute I arrived here, he hs played at the same level. Not up and down, no mistakes. Not more committed against Man United and less concentration against West Bromwich.'

After dropping two points against their nearest rivals, Chelsea put together another incredible run of victories. Norwich City, Aston Villa, Portsmouth (twice), Liverpool, Middlesbrough and Spurs were all brushed aside without even scoring a goal between them as the Premiership dream started to become more and more tangible. Scunthorpe provided little resistance in the FA Cup, even without Terry as Mourinho took the opportunity to rest his skipper for only the third time in 32 matches.

It took some brilliance from Lampard and a bit of luck from Duff to see Chelsea past Manchester United in the semi-final of the League Cup, after the sides had drawn 0–0 in the first leg at Stamford Bridge. The Blues then maintained their four-pronged attack on silverware with a 2–0 win over Birmingham in the FA Cup. Terry scored his seventh goal of the season but he made more headlines for his part in Robert Huth's opening goal in the sixth minute. As Duff's corner curled in from the right, Terry body-checked Huth's marker and the German centre-back rose unchallenged to head home. The captain got one for himself

10 minutes from time when Lampard picked him out with a perfectly flighted cross.

Entering February, the Premiership was the main concern and Manchester United's 4–2 win at Highbury meant that Chelsea could go 11 points clear at the top of the table with a win against Blackburn Rovers. They got off to the perfect start at Ewood Park when Robben drilled the ball under goalkeeper Brad Friedel after five minutes, but the home side's roughhouse tactics forced the Dutch winger out of the game six minutes later. Rovers continued with their aggressive approach and the game became something of a battle.

Things threatened to get out of hand after one hour when Robbie Savage fell in the area under a challenge from Ferreira. Although Cech pulled off a fantastic save to deny Paul Dickov from the penalty spot, the Scottish striker caught the Czech keeper with his follow-up and the Chelsea players weren't happy. Against such hostility Terry and his team-mates dug deep and, despite not playing well, they held out for a 1–0 win to claim another vital three points as they moved towards the business end of the season.

12

February was full of tough games for the Blues. Their winning streak came to an end four days after the victory over Blackburn when they drew 0–0 with Manchester City, but they still managed to maintain their run of clean sheets and even added one more with a 1–0 win at Goodison Park. A week later they suffered their third defeat of the season at St James' Park when their Quadruple dream came crashing to an end. With Terry suspended, they suffered a 1–0 defeat against Newcastle and went out of the FA Cup.

This wasn't the ideal way to prepare for a trip to Barcelona and the Nou Camp and, with three trophies still to fight for, the Chelsea players headed for Spain seeking a return to winning ways. But bad luck continued to dog them. Drogba received a second booking for an innocuous challenge on the Barcelona keeper and was sent off. Chelsea had been leading 1–0 thanks to Juliano Belletti's own goal but, down to 10 men, they lost 2–1.

Having suffered two defeats in one week, Chelsea headed to Cardiff for the League Cup final against

Liverpool, desperate to turn things round. They needed an extra half hour but they achieved it. At the end of a dramatic afternoon, Terry lifted his first major trophy as captain. Liverpool went ahead after 45 seconds, courtesy of a John Arne Riise volley, but Steven Gerrard scored an own goal after 79 minutes to take the game into extra-time. Goals from Drogba and Kezman eventually won the match for Chelsea despite Antonio Nunez's consolation strike for the Reds.

After victory in Cardiff, the Blues notched up a straightforward win over Norwich. Although the Canaries did become the first team to put a Premiership goal past Petr Cech since before Christmas, they were still beaten 3–1. Then came the visit of Barcelona for the Champions League second leg.

In one of the greatest games in Chelsea's history, the Blues were roared on by probably the loudest Bridge crowd of all time and went 3–0 up inside 20 minutes, with goals from Gudjohnsen, Lampard and Duff. Chelsea were in complete control of the tie but they failed to press home their advantage and Barcelona came back strongly through Ronaldinho. Suddenly the score was 3–2. At half time Mourinho told his players they had nothing to fear and that the game was theirs for the taking. Thanks to Terry his words came true. Duff floated a corner across in the 76th minute and the Chelsea skipper shook off his marker to head home. It was his eighth of the season, his fourth in the Champions League and by far the most valuable goal of his life. Chelsea held on to win 4–2 on the night, 5–4 on aggregate, and they were into the last eight.

Things really were going well for Terry. He was in the

middle of another one of those runs of victories that had typified Chelsea's season. They were top of the league, into the quarter-finals in Europe and they already had a first pot in the trophy cabinet. The Blues captain had also played his part in helping England edge towards the World Cup finals, starting alongside Ferdinand against Northern Ireland and Azerbaijan. In Campbell's absence, the Chelsea defender had helped England to two clean sheets and six points as they took another big step down the road to Germany.

Terry's next big test with Chelsea came with the visit of Bayern Munich, but the Blues had too much quality for the opposition and they won 4–2. Bayern won the return leg in Munich thanks to a couple of late, late goals, but it was of little consolation as Chelsea advanced to the semi-finals to face Liverpool. Before turning their attentions to Liverpool, however, Terry and his team-mates had an appointment with Arsenal in the league. The Gunners were holding on to second place in the Premiership, but they were a massive 11 points behind the leaders. A thrilling game at the Bridge somehow remained goalless and, with only five league games left, Chelsea needed just five points to finally claim the title they craved so desperately.

They returned to winning ways with a 3–1 score-line at home to Fulham 50 years to the day since they won their only previous title. That opened up a 14–point gap over Arsenal. The day got even better for Terry when his outstanding achievements saw him named PFA Player of the Year at an awards ceremony later that evening. 'It is unbelievable and the ultimate accolade to be voted for by your fellow professionals whom you play against week in and week out,' he said. The Chelsea captain was the first defender to win the award since Paul McGrath in 1993, the first Englishman to win since Teddy Sheringham in 2001 and the first Blues player ever to collect the prestigious accolade.

Chelsea were at home for the first game in their Champions League semi-final against Liverpool. The match was dominated by defenders and, while Terry snuffed out the threat at one end, Carragher did the same at the other. With the game ending goalless, the tie would have to be settled at Anfield, but before Chelsea's date with their European destiny they had the opportunity to win the league.

Mourinho's side had long looked like champions and at the Reebok Stadium on Saturday, 30 April 2005 they confirmed it. Bolton were in typically muscular mood and they dominated the first half with their aggression and physical presence. Terry was even caught by an un-intentional elbow from Kevin Davies just before half-time and played the remainder of the game with impaired vision. But this was not a time to be without an inspirational captain and, after a rollicking at the interval, Chelsea came out and played the quality football that had taken them to the top.

The midfield started to compete and managed to gain control. Appropriately enough, it was Lampard who scored the goals that gave Chelsea a 2–0 win, three points and the Premiership trophy. 'This is the best feeling ever,' Terry said after the game. 'We've worked so hard all season for it, and to have done it with three games to spare allows us to go into Tuesday's semi-final fully focused on that.'

With the league title in the bag, Chelsea could concentrate on the match at Anfield. Liverpool were equally fired up for the big night, however, and with two of the best defences in Europe squaring up, it would take something special to break the deadlock. Sadly for the Blues, that something special came from Luis Garcia with plenty of help from the linesman. There were only four minutes on the clock when Steven Gerrard played Milan Baros in on goal. The Czech striker lifted the ball over his compatriot Petr Cech but fell under the goalkeeper's challenge. The ball dropped to Garcia in the area and he struck it towards the goal. William Gallas was back covering and appeared to clear the effort before it crossed the line, but after consulting his linesman, the referee made his decision in Liverpool's favour and the Reds were ahead 1–0.

It proved to be the only goal of the match. Looking back at Liverpool's European campaign, it seemed their name was on the trophy from day one, and they eventually claimed the big prize on a memorable night in Istanbul, but that did little to console the Chelsea players. 'William Gallas was in the way of the ball from where the linesman was, but he gave it, which was a bad decision,' Terry said of the controversial incident. 'If you're not sure, then don't give a goal.'

Chelsea picked themselves up for the last home game of the campaign and, after beating Charlton 1–0 with Makelele scoring his only goal of the season in the last minute, John Terry was presented with the Premiership trophy. It was his final contribution for the season. Chelsea then beat Manchester United 3–1 and drew 1–1 with

Newcastle in the captain's absence. He went under the surgeon's knife to resolve a problem with his toes that had forced him to have pain-killing injections before games. He would also have to miss England's summer tour of America but with his injury sorted out, things could only get better.

13

As well as having his skipper fully fit and pain free, Jose Mourinho had made other moves to significantly strengthen his squad in the summer of 2005. Asier Del Horno, Shaun Wright-Phillips and Michael Essien joined the club for a combined fee of over £50 million. With the backing of one of the richest men on the planet, the best team in the land were looking to stay ahead of the chasing pack.

Chelsea began the season by beating Arsenal 2–1 in the FA Community Shield. It was the first time Terry had been on the winning side against the Gunners in a domestic match, and it served to further enforce the psychological advantage the champions held over their London rivals. Then they made an extraordinary start to their defence of the Premiership, winning their first nine league games, scoring 23 goals and only conceding three as they kept six clean sheets.

However, the captain of the champions still faced tough competition from Rio Ferdinand and Sol Campbell in the fight for an England place. Terry did nothing spectacular in his 45 minute run out against Denmark, but after his substitution England fell apart on their way to a shocking 4–1 defeat in Copenhagen.

England, badly needing six points, now faced Wales and Northern Ireland. Terry missed both games due to a knee injury, but Joe Cole's goal secured a 1–0 win in Cardiff. Four days later Eriksson's troops succumbed to a David Healy strike to lose in Belfast, as Terry's importance to the team became increasingly obvious.

The Champions League brought Chelsea head to head with Liverpool once again. The Blues only managed a draw at Anfield, but their next league game was at the same venue four days later, and this time they turned on the style to triumph 4–1. After a week on Merseyside, Terry once again left his club to play for England and, in the World Cup qualifier against Austria, the Chelsea skipper found himself lining up alongside Sol Campbell in defence; Rio Ferdinand was the odd-man out.

David Beckham was sent off after 59 minutes and, although the armband went to Michael Owen, the Chelsea captain helped rally the troops and hold on for victory. Campbell got an injury, so Terry was joined by Ferdinand at the heart of the defence, and England claimed top spot in Group Six with a 2–1 win.

Having helped England to the World Cup and further enhanced his increasingly secure position in the England team, Terry helped guide Chelsea to even more success. They trounced Bolton 5–1, and then Real Betis 4–0 to put them ahead of Liverpool on goal difference at the top of Group G in the Champions League. The demolition of the Spanish side gave the Blues to 13 goals from three games, and buried the 'boring' tag they'd picked up after having to grind out some results. But after nine straight Premiership wins Chelsea suffered the first blip in what looked like their inevitable road to the title, drawing 1–1 away to Everton.

Things got worse as the Blues lost to Charlton on penalties in the League Cup, despite Terry claiming his first goal of the season. Although Chelsea rallied in their next game to beat Blackburn in the league, the manner of the win showed Mourinho's team weren't at their best, conceding two goals on their way to a 4–2 victory. And their sudden poor form was emphasised as they lost their next two games 1–0, away to Real Betis and then Manchester United.

Their first Premiership defeat of the season left Chelsea 10 points clear at the top of the table, but before trying to turn around their fortunes at club level the Blues' players joined their countries, and Terry had a game against Argentina. With only seven months to go until the World Cup, a game against the South Americans gave Eriksson the chance to see how his side measured up against some world-class opposition. England twice came from behind to win 3–2, and the result added to the belief that 2006 would be the year when England won the grandest prize in football.

The break from club action worked spectacularly to Chelsea's advantage for a change. The players returned rejuvenated from internationals and resumed their early season form rather than the stuttering play that had brought just one win from the five games just before England's win over Argentina. Terry was happy at the heart of a defence that kept six successive clean sheets in all competitions, but he also chipped in at the other end with the only goal of the game against both Middlesbrough and Wigan as the Blues won 10 Premiership games on the trot.

The highlight of Chelsea's incredible run was a 2–0 win over Arsenal at Highbury as Mourinho maintained a psychological edge over one of his closest domestic rivals. Meanwhilke, in Europe, Chelsea qualified for the knock-out stages with a 2–0 win over Anderlecht in Belgium before a 0–0 draw with Liverpool which meant Terry's side finished second in the group.

Chelsea were totally dominant in the Premiership and had an 11-point lead at the top of the table moving into the World Cup year. Terry was an immovable rock of consistency at the heart of the Blues' defence, helping to drive them towards what everyone in SW6 hoped would be a second successive title. Victory over Sunderland at the Stadium of Light saw their lead stretch to 16 points. Terry then helped his team to a Merseyside double, beating Liverpool and Everton at Stamford Bridge as the Blues returned to winning ways. Mourinho's captain even scored his fourth goal of the season against the Toffees in a 4–1 win, taking Chelsea to the fifth round of the FA Cup after a replay. But rather than providing the springboard to launch another run of victories, the Blues surprisingly crashed to a humiliating 3–0 defeat away to Middlesbrough.

After falling at the semi-final stage in the previous two Champions League seasons, Terry was desperate to lead his team to the 2006 final in Paris. But first they had top overcome Barcelona. The whole of Europe was looking forward to this one, but the game proved more than a little disappointing for the Chelsea captain as he scored an own-goal in Barcelona's 2–1 win at Stamford Bridge. Terry then had a busy fortnight before the trip to Catalonia winning all three three games, two with Chelsea and one with England, where he was once again selected alongside Ferdinand. But he couldn't make it four in a row at the Nou Camp where a 1–1 draw ended the Blues' European dream for another season.

Devastated, Terry and his team-mates returned to London knowing they had to lift themselves for two big derby matches. They continued their domination of Spurs with a 2–1 win, stretching their unbeaten run against them to 32 league games since 1990. But a week later they lost their west London bragging rights being beaten 1–0 at Craven Cottage. But Chelsea were still top of the table, and they kept their hopes of a domestic double alive three days later when they saw off Newcastle at the Bridge in the FA Cup quarter-final, Terry volleying home the winning goal from Duff's corner after just four minutes.

Chelsea continued their march towards a second Premiership trophy with four wins and a draw in their next five games. Terry took his tally for the season to seven with a goal against West Ham and another against Bolton the following week. Then a 3–0 home win over Everton brought the title within touching distance, but before they could retain their trophy Chelsea faced an FA Cup semi-final against Liverpool. It was the tenth time in two seasons that the clubs had faced each other, and the Blues had lost only one of those encounters: the Champions League semi-final second leg at Anfield. However, Rafa Benitez's side edged their way into the final with a 2–1 win at Old Trafford and, for the second year running, Terry had to watch Liverpool win a trophy that he had hoped to lift.

There was little time for him to dwell on the departure of the Double dream as Chelsea next entertained Manchester United, needing just a draw to secure the Premiership. The Blues wrapped up their second Premiership in spectacular style, beating their nearest rivals 3–0. Terry was imperious at the back, and the only trouble he had from the visitors was when Wayne Rooney accidentally caught him on the shin after seven minutes, opening up a gash which later required 10 stitches, keeping the Blues' skipper out of the final two league games of the season. But Terry had been raised to never show his opponents any sign of weakness, and he endured the pain to guide his team to victory and the title.

'There was no way I was coming off,' the limping defender told *Sky Sports*. 'What a season! To retain the title is absolutely fantastic. We found it more difficult going to places and getting results but we dug in and did it again. That's the best atmosphere I've ever seen at the Bridge. That's a great result against a great side.'

With the triumphant return of the Premiership trophy to Stamford Bridge, Terry now turned his thoughts to another, even bigger prize. England's World Cup preparations had yet again been undermined by injuries and, most worrying, the first-choice strike-force of Michael Owen and Wayne Rooney were battling for fitness.

Terry, now a dad to the twins Summer Rose and Georgie John, celebrated fatherhood with England's second goal in the 3–1 win over Hungary. The goal gave Terry a boost with the World Cup drawing ever closer, as did the 6–0 drubbing of Jamaica four days later. And with Rooney still on the sidelines, Peter Crouch advanced his claims for a place in the team with a hat-trick against the Caribbean side.

It was a first World Cup for Terry. In the four years since the last tournament he had become one of the first names on the team sheet, and he couldn't wait for the competition to begin. England fans were concerned when he limped out of the Jamaica match after 36 minutes, but it was merely a precautionary measure and seven days later he lined up against Paraguay for the Group B opener. It wasn't a great start. In the soaring temperatures England laboured to a 1–0 win over the South Americans, thanks to an own goal.

Eriksson made just one change, bringing in Jamie Carragher for the injured Neville at right back to face Trinidad five days later, and with an evening kick-off the weather could provide no excuses. The World Cup first-timers proved a resilient bunch but England won 2–0 to ensure their place in the knock out stages. Rooney returned with his side needing just a draw to top Group B, and looking for a first win over Sweden for 38 years. Eriksson's team started the game well and, during the first half, they played their best football of the tournament, taking a 1–0 lead into the break thanks to a wonder goal from Joe Cole. But they faded after the interval for the third match in succession, and twice conceded the lead. It was a shambolic end to the game, but the point secured England's place at the top of the group and meant that they would meet Ecuador in the next round, whilse Sweden faced their German hosts.

Terry hadn't been at the top of his form but he gave a

man-of-the-match display against Ecuador to help England into the quarter-finals. Still under-performing as a team, Eriksson's side won 1–0 with much of the credit for the 'nil' belonging to the Chelsea captain. The England goal again came from a set piece as Beckham curled home a trademark free kick after an hour. The sweltering lunchtime heat was responsible for the England skipper being sick briefly after scoring, and when he was substituted four minutes from time the armband moved to Terry who was already turning in a captain's performance.

Now England faced a formidable task against Portugal. Eriksson changed his tactics and left Rooney to plough a lone furrow up front, and the fiery Manchester United forward grew increasingly frustrated. His temperament boiled over in the 62nd minute and he was sent off for stamping on Ricardo Carvalho. Playing the remainder of the game with 10 men, England failed to break down Scolari's side and, with Terry remaining immovable at the back, the scoreless game drifted towards penalties. A dismal tournament was rounded off as Lampard, Gerrard and Carragher all had their spot kicks saved. Portugal won the shoot-out 3–1 and England's World Cup was over.

14

Sven-Goran Eriksson departed after the World Cup exit and David Beckham stood down as England captain. The new man in charge, Steve McClaren, phoned John Terry and offered him the armband. 'It is the ultimate honour to be the captain of your country and I am very proud to be given this great opportunity. It is an incredible challenge and one I am looking forward to very much,' Terry said.

The new skipper got off to a great start when he scored in his first game with the armband, a 4–0 win over Greece at Old Trafford on 16 August 2006. His was the opening goal after 14 minutes, nodding in a flick-on from Stewart Downing. After the match he revealed that his predecessor had been in touch: 'I had a text message before the game from Becks wishing me good luck in my first game as captain,' Terry said. 'It was the perfect start for me. It has been a dream come true for me, especially scoring the goal. I felt so proud leading the team out and then singing the national anthem as captain. I am more than happy with the result and with the performance.'

England went one better in the first competitive match of the McClaren era when they beat Andorra 5–0 at Old Trafford in the European Championship qualifying campaign. England further cemented their place at the top of Group E with a 1–0 win in Macedonia but struggled in their next two games, as Macedonia held on for a draw at Old Trafford, and Croatia won 2–0 in Zagreb four days later.

On the domestic scene Chelsea looked well equipped to defend their title having recruited Germany captain Michael Ballack, the 2004 European Footballer of the Year Andriy Shevchenko, the England left-back Ashley Cole and promising youngsters like John Obi Mikel, Salomon Kalou and Khalid Boulahrouz. Despite losing the FA Community Shield to Liverpool in Cardiff and falling 2–1 to Middlesbrough at the Riverside, Chelsea put together a run of six successive victories through August and September putting them at the top of the Premiership and in control of their European future. Terry even scored the Blues' first competitive goal of the season, heading home Arjen Robben's free-kick after 11 minutes on the way to a 3–0 win over Manchester City at the Bridge.

He was proving himself a Captain Marvel for both club and country, and he led England to victories over Andorra and Macedonia before returning to the blue shirt of Chelsea. Winning can become a habit, and so it proved for Terry and his team-mates as they put aside Charlton and Werder Bremen, before delivering a potential death blow to one of their title rivals, beating Liverpool 1–0 to leave the Reds eight points adrift of joint Premiership leaders Chelsea and Manchester United.

The skipper was missing as the Blues overcame their west London rivals Fulham at Craven Cottage, but he returned to the side for the trip to Sofia where Levski were beaten 3–1 to keep Terry on course for some European silverware. After the game in Bulgaria the Barking-born defender experienced his first blip of the season as September drew to a close. Chelsea dropped their first home points of the campaign drawing 1–1 with Aston Villa.

Chelsea's next match was away to Reading, where two horrific injuries to Petr Cech and Carlo Cudicini meant that Terry played out the final minutes of a 1–0 win in goal. Cech fractured his skull when Stephen Hunt's knee caught him on the temple in the first minute of the match, and Cudicini was later knocked unconscious in a collision with Ibrahima Sonko. After a long delay the Chelsea skipper took the gloves, and he retreated between the sticks where he survived the last few minutes without the home side managing to test him.

Fortunately Cech made a full recovery and he was back playing in the Chelsea goal by late January. But the scale of the injury meant he needed delicate neurosurgery to relieve pressure on his skull. Missing arguably the world's best goalkeeper, the Blues took on the champions of Europe in the next match when Barcelona travelled to London.

Terry led his side to a fine 1–0 win over the Catalans, followed by three wins in a week as Chelsea made light of their first choice keeper's absence. But the fine form couldn't last forever and, in the return game in Barcelona, Chelsea failed to win for the first time in six games as a scrappy affair ended 2–2. Mourinho's men showed a lot of character to come from behind twice and the result left them one point away from qualification for the knock-out stages, while their opponents languished in third place in Group A.

The match clearly took its toll on the Chelsea players however, and they slipped to their first defeat in 14 games when they faced Spurs five days later. Terry was sent off for the first time in his club career in a 2–1 loss. The result of the dismissal was a one-match ban, which saw Chelsea without their captain for Aston Villa's visit to Stamford Bridge in the fourth round of the Carling Cup. The Blues made light of his absence on their way to a 4–0 win, and the dominant centre-back returned for the next match where Watford were dispatched by the same score as Chelsea extended their unbeaten run at home to 50 matches under Mourinho.

After notching up yet another impressive milestone at club level, Terry again turned his attentions to international duty and a trip to Amsterdam for a friendly against the Netherlands. England put in a much-improved performance against the Dutch in a 1–1 draw, only being robbed of victory by Rafael van der Vaart's late strike.

Chelsea, on the other hand, still weren't back to their formidable best as they followed a workmanlike 1–0 win over West Ham by losing 1–0 to Werder Bremen. It was hardly the ideal preparation as the Blues psyched themselves up for a visit to Old Trafford to face their only real opposition for the Premiership title. Chelsea lay in second place, three points behind Manchester United and on the day there was little to choose between the two teams as the match ended with honours even, 1–1.

The performance raised hopes that Terry and company were in a good position to kick on but, just as their form seemed to be returning, they lost their skipper to a back injury. He was ruled out for nearly two months, missing 13 games as Chelsea fell further behind their rivals at the top of the table.

After the draw at Old Trafford, Terry did help Chelsea keep a clean sheet to win 1–0 in a tricky trip to Bolton's Reebok Stadium, and although he was missing the 2–0 win over Levski Sofia that guaranteed them top spot in Group A of the Champions League, he managed to return for a 1–1 draw with Arsenal and a win over Newcastle at Stamford Bridge to keep the pressure on Alex Ferguson's team.

It was after the victory over the Magpies that Terry's problem came to light, and his absence was felt immediately as Chelsea's oncemiserly defence began to haemorrhage goals. The outlook was bleak, with some experts predicting the England defender could be out for three months after surgery in France to remove a 'sequestrated lumbar intervertebral disc', which in layman's terms equates to a slipped disc. Amazingly, Terry returned to Premiership action within five weeks of his operation.

Chelsea had stuttered on. They were through to the final of the League Cup and the fourth round of the FA Cup, but they had picked up just 18 from a possible 27 points in the Premiership, leaving them six points behind Manchester United and in danger of relinquishing the title they had fought so hard for the previous two seasons.

Terry finally returned at the start of February, coming on for the last five minutes against Charlton. There was still time to close the title gap. With Terry and Cech reunited on the pitch for the first time since October, the Blues continued their winning ways winning 1–0 before John was forced to miss his first England match since taking the armband for his country. Having played only five minutes of competitive football in the past eight weeks, Terry wasn't up to the rigours of international football and Steven Gerrard stepped up as captain for the friendly at Old Trafford, where Andres Iniesta's second half strike secured a 1–0 win for Spain and England were booed off at the final whistle.

Terry was finally ready for 90 minutes the following Saturday as Middlesbrough made the trip to west London. Gareth Southgate's team were no match for a Blues side approaching full strength and were despatched 3–0. Norwich City offered even less resistance in the FA Cup, losing 4–0, and it looked like Mourinho's team were hitting form at just the right time as they entertained his old club Porto in the knockout stage of the Champions League.

A 1–1 draw in the first leg in Portugal wasn't too bad as the away goal gave Chelsea the advantage heading into the home tie, but the bad news was that Terry injured an ankle ligament and, after being substituted, left the stadium on crutches. With the League Cup Final only four days away nobody gave him a hope of facing Arsenal at the Millennium Stadium, but once again the imposing centre-back surprised medical opinion and delighted his fans with a swift return to the pitch.

Having made a second remarkable return to fitness, Terry had hoped that his injury problems were behind him but, diving for a header on the Cardiff pitch, he was knocked out by Abou Diaby's right foot as Arsenal's French

midfielder attempted to clear a corner. The blow left the defensive colossus out cold and with some memory loss. Terry's final was over and he was forced out of the next three matches, but ironically he was back playing before Diaby, who had injured his ankle in the collision.

Fortunately, the injury to the captain didn't stop the Blues adding to their trophy cabinet as two goals from Didier Drogba helped Chelsea back from a goal down to win 2–1. A great game was sullied by a late brawl, which saw John Obi Mikel and two Arsenal players sent off. Terry was taken to hospital for precautionary scans on his head, but once he was given the all-clear he was able to join in the celebrations at the Millennium Stadium and late into the night when the team got back to London.

Forced to sit out the next three games, Terry had to watch from the sidelines again. Increasingly accustomed to playing without their captain, Mourinho's team beat Portsmouth in the league and Porto in Europe before Spurs exploited some defensive frailty, going 3–1 up in an FA Cup tie at the Bridge, before drawing 3–3. After seeing such an inept performance at the back against their London rivals, the Chelsea fans gave Terry a hero's welcome when they travelled to Manchester for the game against City.

Sitting nine points behind Manchester United, Chelsea were under immense pressure, but with Terry back at the heart of the defence there was a renewed confidence that the Premiership title, and possibly even the Champions League and FA Cup, could still be added to the League Cup. The wins kept coming for Chelsea. Sheffield United were brushed aside in the league and Spurs were shown the true resolve of Mourinho's players in the FA Cup replay, as superb goals from Andriy Shevchenko and Shaun Wright-Phillips guided the Blues to a 2–1 win and a place in the semi-finals.

With games arriving thick and fast, it was time again for Terry to join up with England as they tried to rescue their teetering Euro 2008 qualifying campaign. Two away games against Israel and Andorra presented the perfect opportunity to turn things around in Group E. Tel Aviv is a tough place to go and McClaren's men laboured to a 0–0 draw. They had scored just one goal in their last five winless games, representing their worst run of form in front of goal since the spring of 1981 when Ron Greenwood was still manager. Things were much easier in the next game as Terry and his compatriots took on Andorra in Barcelona, where two goals from Steven Gerrard brace and one from David Nugent secured a 3–0 win.

After helping his country to four valuable points, Terry concentrated on trying to win more silverware for Chelsea.

15

Chelsea hadn't given up hope of snatching the title from Manchester United and, even though they had to fight right up to the death to beat Watford, Salomon Kalou's last-minute winner meant they reduced the gap to six points. With eight games in 24 days coming up in April, Terry and his team-mates would have no time to rest.

They were quickly back in action in the Champions League quarter-final against Valencia. A 1–1 draw at Stamford Bridge handed the advantage to the Spanish side but, after overcoming Spurs in the league, Chelsea won 2–1 in the Mestella to secure a place in the last four, where they again faced Liverpool.

Before continuing their European adventure, Chelsea maintained their bid for domestic honours gaining revenge for the league defeat at White Hart Lane with a 1–0 win over Spurs and then bookied a place in the FA Cup Final after beating Blackburn 2–1 at Old Trafford. The Blues made it nine consecutive Premiership wins when they beat West Ham 4–1 away, but that fine run came to an end at Newcastle when they were held to a 0–0 draw. And still the matches came.

Terry led his side to a 1–0 win in the first leg of the Champions League semi-final at home, setting them up perfectly for the return game a week later in Liverpool. At Anfield, the Blues were forced to settle for a penalty shoot-out after losing 1–0 on the night. It was a disaster. Frank Lampard was the only Chelsea player to score as Liverpool ran out 4–1 winners in the spot-kick lottery.

The disappointing European campaign had also taken its toll on Chelsea's title aspirations. They followed up the draw against Newcastle with a 2–2 draw at home to Bolton in between the two legs of the Champions League semi-final, before a 1–1 draw away to Arsenal handed the title to Manchester United. In their next game the Red Devils headed to Stamford Bridge as champions.

Chelsea gave Alex Fergson's team a guard of honour, similar to that which they had received in the northwest 12 months previously. But having relinquished their title, the Blues were in no mood to surrender their two-year unbeaten run at home and held Manchester United to a 0–0 draw. The much-anticipated match between the league's top two was a bit of an anti-climax, and both sides seemed content to save themselves for their next meeting 10 days later at the newly refurbished Wembley Stadium.

The 2007 FA Cup Final was special to most people because it was the first at Wembley since 2000, but it was momentous for Terry because it was the first time he started in a Cup Final team. And he was even more delighted to lead his side out and finally, after nearly two hours of a finely poised match, to lift the oldest cup in football.

The excellent form of Didier Drogba had helped maintain Chelsea's long and gutsy challenge on all four

fronts, and it was apt that he should score the winner in the Cup Final, slotting past Edwin van der Sar after a delightful one-two with Frank Lampard four minutes from the end of extra time. It was his 33rd goal of an incredible season, and meant that the Blues picked up the last piece of domestic silverware.

It had been a difficult year for Terry because he suffered with injuries and ill-fortune, but he still had international commitments as he led England out for their first game at the new Wembley. The defender made history once again as he scored his country's first goal under the arch at the incredible new stadium, when the home team drew 1–1 with Brazil. The friendly was followed by a 3–0 win against Estonia in Tallinn, and England consolidated their position in Group E of their European Championship qualifying campaign. The three points left McClaren's side in fourth place, but only three points off top spot; qualification was back in their own hands.

More good news followed. Terry and Toni were married that summer and his agent negotiated a new deal, allegedly worth £135,000 a week, making him the highest-paid player in the history of English football. The five-year deal was worth more than £7 million a year and had taken months to sort out, but everyone connected with Chelsea was delighted to get it signed.

The hierarchy at Stamford Bridge were less happy with what they were seeing on the pitch. Mourinho was winning trophies every season, that was expected, but Roman Abramovich expected to see victory achieved with more swagger and style, and after his massive investment he didn't think he was getting that. Rumours of a split between manager and chairman started to circulate. Could Chelsea would part company with their most successful manager ever?

The story of Mourinho's exit broke as journalists waited outside a cinema in a Fulham Broadway shopping centre where the club's DVD, *Blue Revolution*, was premiered, ironically telling the story of the Special One's time at the club. His troubled expression as he brushed past journalists afterwards signified he was well aware that matters were coming to a head. Speculation quickly began to spread that Mourinho had been whisked straight to Stamford Bridge for emergency talks with Abramovich and that he'd stormed out of the club, having already warned his players of his departure earlier in the day. Later that night the Blues eventually announced that the greatest manager in Chelsea history had 'left by mutual consent'.

The Special One was so loved by his players that several, including Didier Drogba, later admitted they felt like quitting west London. However, it wasn't long before some newspapers also started carrying stories of betrayal, that Mourinho had been stabbed in the back. Even Terry was caught up in the accusations. There were reports he had fallen out with Mourinho and even suggestions that the captain had somehow played a part in his manager's unexpected exit. Similar accusations surfaced again a year or two later when Claude Makelele claimed in his autobiography that Terry was partly to blame for Mourinho's demise. It's an accusation that Terry is determined to counter.

'It's bizarre because he knows the real truth,' he said. 'If anything, I was one of three players phoning Roman at one or two in the morning when I heard Jose had been sacked and asking for him to be kept on. I was speaking to Peter Kenyon, Roman and Eugene [Tenebaum, a club director] and hoping we could keep him. Myself, Lamps and Didier were fighting for him. I spoke to Mourinho and he's totally fine with it. He sent me a text and I called him straight back and we spoke about the situation. We know what happened, the relationship between him and the football club. They parted on mutual terms. If I had that much power I would have changed an awful lot of things at this football club a long time ago! No one player is bigger than any football club and I'm no different. I have my opinion, the same as Lamps and people like that, but nothing else. I wish I had that much power but I haven't!'

16

Whatever the truth, it is fair to say that Mourinho's departure left behind a squad in mourning. And it left John Terry with a tough job to bring everyone back together. In a way, the announcement that Avram Grant, Chelsea's Director of Football, would take over the reins gave Terry the power to do exactly that. Grant was given little respect by the press, and during his tenure he was always seen as a stop-gap but his amiable personality and lack of ego meant he was willing to leave things – including tactics, training schedules and the matchday routine – largely the same as under Mourinho.

For some critics it showed a lack of leadership, and reports regularly suggested that it was Terry who effectively became Chelsea's manager for the rest of the season as he led team talks and gained a more powerful influence on the training field. This view was strengthened in the Carling Cup Final against Spurs in February 2008 when the match went to extra-time and Grant seemed happy to take a back seat at the end of 90 minutes, leaving Terry to fill the gap. Spurs went on to lift the trophy, winning 2–1, a result that added to the jibes. But Grant's record as Chelsea manager stands up to scrutiny because, despite the off-field rows, dressing-room rifts and stuttering performances, he was able to re-ignite their title challenge and take the team all the way to the Champions League Final, something not even the Special One could do.

Grant's very first game in charge was something of a no-win situation, an away match at Manchester United but, after losing that game 2–0, Chelsea recovered well. Highlights in the league included a 6–0 thrashing of Manchester City at the Bridge, a thumping 4–0 win over West Ham at Upton Park and a 1–0 victory at Sunderland where Terry scored his only goal of the season.

In fact, having been well behind in the title race at one stage, Chelsea now pushed United all the way to the final game when the Blues needed to beat Bolton and hope United drew or lost against Wigan to be crowned champions. It was always going to be a tall order and when United won 2–0 and Chelsea drew 1–1 the dream was over once again, although Grant is entitled to claim some kind of moral victory given the hurdles that were put in his way.

The Israeli also worked his magic in the Champions League with many notable achievements, including finishing top of the group before beating Olympiakos and Fenerbahce, and then overturning Liverpool in the semi-final. Chelsea took a 3–2 victory at Stamford Bridge after extra-time in the second leg, thanks to two goals from Drogba and one from Lampard. The victory set up a final to savour because Chelsea were up against Manchester United in Moscow.

The much-maligned Grant knew only victory would give him any chance of keeping his job, despite the way he had been able to steady a ship that had looked ready to sink. And none of the players in the squad were under any illusions about just how much the Champions League Final meant to owner Roman Abramovich, hungry for a win in his home town. His dream and reputation were at stake.

The nerves certainly showed in the opening stages because United were rampant, dominating midfield and going ahead through a Cristiano Ronaldo header. But the way Chelsea roared back speaks volumes about captain Terry and his team-mates. They equalized just before half-time when Michael Essien's deflected shot eventually fell for Lampard to score. Chelsea dominated after the break, but the nearest they came to scoring was when Didier Drogba's 77th-minute shot came back off the post.

Things got worse in extra time when Drogba was sent off for slapping Nemanja Vidić. With the leading scorer absent, Grant asked Terry to be one of Chelsea's five penalty takers. 'I was never going to say no,' he later admitted.

The final shoot-out saw Ronaldo, of all people, scuff his kick and it seemed the trophy was coming, at last, to Stamford Bridge. Frank Lampard did his part by putting Chelsea 3–2 ahead and, seconds later, with the score 4–4, it fell to Terry to win the Champions League trophy for his club. Would Mr Chelsea score the winning goal to get his hands on the European Cup?

Terry looked confident but, just at the crucial moment, he slipped and sent the ball skidding past Edwin van der Sar's left-hand post. The Chelsea skipper was inconsolable and, although history will tell you it was van der Sar's save from Nicolas Anelka's spot-kick that won the trophy for United 6–5, the Blues' captain shed tears at the final whistle and has never forgotten the feeling. 'I still think about it every day, probably 20, 30, 40 times a day, I promise you,' he told a Sky documentary team in September 2009. 'When I wake up it's on my mind, when I go to training and when we practice penalties at the training ground. It's such a bad memory for me and the lads.'

That moment of heartbreak has shaped Terry's life and career ever since. He still has the shirt and boots he wore that day in Moscow displayed in a glass case at his house in Surrey, and he gazes at them from time to time to remind him of how it felt – and to inspire him to put it right. 'It's my way of dealing with it,' he said. 'And if we do get to another final I will volunteer to take one again. I still practice in training. With the group of players we've got I'm probably sixth, seventh or eighth in line because we have so many good penalty takers. But on that night in Moscow the manager asked me to step up and there was no way I was going to turn it down. If I get asked again I'll take one, too.'

Unfortunately for Grant, defeat in the Champions League Final was the end of the road for him. After just eight months in charge, he was unceremoniously sacked as Chelsea again looked for the elusive man who could fulfil the chairman's desires to win the major trophies with exhilarating football.

With the pain of Moscow still in their bones, Chelsea players started a new campaign under the guidance of Luiz Felipe Scolari, who was still the manager of Portugal and halfway through the Euro 2008 campaign. No one cold argue with his credentials. This was the man who had won the World Cup with Brazil and guided Portugal to the final of Euro 2004 and the semi-finals of the World Cup in 2006, beating England on penalties on both occasions. There was a feeling at Stamford Bridge that he was the man to guide them to glory.

Terry had been named UEFA's Defender of the Year for 2008 and been confirmed as England captain when Fabio Capello took charge of the national side. Now he dreamed of club success under Scolari, a desire shared by thousands of Blues fans. Yet, incredibly, the dream turned sour within months. Early in the season it seemed Scolari's tactics were destined to take Chelsea to the next level as they beat Portsmouth 4–0 on the opening day with a scintillating display. And after 13 games the 'Blue Brazil' were top of the table. But as other teams began to unpick Scolari's tactics it became clear that the Brazilian had no 'Plan B' and was struggling to come to terms with Premier League football.

A humiliating 3–1 away defeat to Roma, in which Chelsea were abysmal, summed up their problems, and these were underlined by a Carling Cup exit against Burnley. A home defeat against Liverpool – which ended a run of 86 home matches without defeat – saw Scolari now outfoxed by Rafa Benitez and, when the Blues also lost at home to Arsenal, the writing was on the wall. The Scolari honeymoon period was well and truly over. Things got worse over winter as Chelsea were humiliatingly held to a draw by League One side Southend United in the FA Cup before they were crushed 3–0 at Old Trafford by Manchester United.

With Chelsea outside of the Champions League places, not even captain Terry could turn things around, although he admits he was stunned when Chelsea eventually lost patience and sacked Scolari on 9 February 2009, just seven months after his arrival in west London. But if Terry was worried his club was about to implode, his concerns were quickly eased after the club appointed Guus Hiddink as their new manager.

Ray Wilkins kept the ship afloat until Hiddink's arrival by guiding his team to victory at Watford in the FA Cup, a win that heralded an amazing turnaround. The choice of Hiddink was controversial because he was also manager of Russia and had agreed to take the job only as a personal favour to Roman Abramovich on a part-time and short-term basis until the end of the season. But the Dutchman quickly made his presence felt as he worked wonders off the pitch to heal the wounds of a team ripped apart by in-fighting. With Hiddink at the helm, and Drogba back on form, Chelsea put together four straight league wins, including a hard-fought 1–0 victory at Villa Park on his first day in charge. In all they won 11 of their last 13 Premiership matches that season, including a superb 4–1 victory over Arsenal at the Emirates, and also progressed to the semi-finals of the Champions League and a tie against Barcelona.

It was a quite remarkable turnaround, and with Terry working overtime to bring back the kind of team spirit that had made Chelsea almost unbeatable under Jose Mourinho, it looked like the old Blues were finally back in town. The team's Champions League run included victories over Juventus and Liverpool, and when Chelsea drew 0–0 in Barcelona in the semi-final first leg, with their captain putting in an outstanding display, it seemed they were destined for their second final in two years despite all the off-field trauma. But it wasn't to be. They had a string of penalty appeals turned down in the second leg before Andres Iniesta scored in the third minute of injury time to equalize Essien's early goal. Barcelona went into the final on the away goals rule.

All that was left for Chelsea, after that disappointment, was the 2009 FA Cup at the end of May. Terry had already made a big impact in Chelsea's league revival, scoring in a 2–1 victory over Wigan to become the club's highest-scoring defender of all time before making his 400th appearance during a 3–1 victory over Fulham. Just days after the Barcelona nightmare he had also guided the Blues to a thumping 4–1 victory over Arsenal that guaranteed Champions League football the following season.

Although Chelsea publicly refused to give up the title, everyone at the Bridge knew that the FA Cup was their only real chance of glory, which made their semi-final against the Gunners even more important. Fortunately, Arsène Wenger's men were unable to gain revenge and the Blues won 2–1 at Wembley thanks to goals from Florent Malouda and a revitalized Drogba.

That set up a final against Everton, a match that Hiddink made clear would be his last in charge despite the overwhelming wish from players and fans for him to stay. Chelsea said goodbye to Hiddink with a dominant display against Everton, even though they conceded a goal to Louis Saha after just 25 seconds. Malouda then crossed for Drogba to equalize and finally, in the 70th minute, Lampard unleashed a stunning, winning goal from 25 yards.

The scene in the Chelsea dressing room was something special and Terry quickly spoke of his desire for a new start, a new Blue era. 'It was fantastic in the dressing room,' he said. 'The manager pulled all the lads to one side. What was said is very private but it was emotional. It was a great farewell. We gave him a gift last night with a message on the back of a watch and a framed shirt. It was a really good night and a really good day.'

Speculation that Terry could leave Chelsea to join the revolution at Manchester City dogged him throughout the summer of 2009, but City's three bids were firmly rejected and Terry has since signed a new contract at the Bridge, and insisted he never had any intention of leaving. 'I'm delighted to have signed a new contract,' he said when his five-year deal was announced. 'It was something that happened very quickly.' Terry's overwhelming wish now is for a period of stability at Stamford Bridge and the signs are good after former AC Milan boss Carlo Ancelotti was appointed as Hiddink's successor in the summer of 2009. Chelsea's early season forms suggests that they are still the team to beat.

Terry's performances as England captain had also been outstanding and helped Fabio Capello's side qualify for the World Cup finals in confident style. A record of eight victories in their opening eight qualifying games was more than enough to send England to South Africa, a trip finally secured by a stunning 5–1 victory over Croatia at Wembley. 'After the game when we beat Croatia you could see what it meant to us players, especially after the experience of not qualifying for Euro 2008,' said Terry. 'The determination we've shown this campaign to get the belief has been fantastic. It's a good achievement.'

JOHN TERRY

Unfortunately, Terry was again in the news for the wrong reasons when newspapers carried stories of an affair with the girlfriend of ex-team-mate Wayne Bridge. The possible disruption in the England dressing room was enough for Capello to strip the Chelsea player of his country's captaincy, handing the armband to Rio Ferdinand. But Terry has shown his ability to come back from off-field crises before, and no one would bet against him being one of England's heroes in the 2010 World Cup finals.